THE
FRANKLIN
COMES
HOME

THE FRANKLIN COMES HOME

A. A. HOEHLING

BLUEJACKET BOOKS

NAVAL INSTITUTE PRESS
Annapolis, Maryland

Originally published by Hawthorn Books, Inc.
First Bluejacket Books printing, 1997

Library of Congress Cataloging-in-Publication Data
Hoehling, A. A. (Adolph A.)
    The Franklin comes home / A.A. Hoehling.
        p.   cm. — (Bluejacket books)
    Originally published : New York : Hawthorn Books, 1974
    Includes bibliographical references and index.
    ISBN 1-55750-371-0 (pbk. : alk. paper)
    1. Franklin (Aircraft carrier).   2. World War, 1939–1945—Naval operations, American.   I. Title.   II. Series.
D774.F7H64   1997
940.54'5973—dc21   97-45

Printed in the United States of America on acid-free paper ∞

04 03 02 01 00 99 98 97   8 7 6 5 4 3 2 1

To the 704 officers and men
who brought the *Franklin* home
this book is dedicated

"Abandon? Hell! We're still afloat!"
—Leslie Gehres, March 19, 1945

CONTENTS

PREFACE

The United States Navy entered World War II with 8 aircraft carriers. Before peace was restored, 113 additional carriers had been commissioned, which compared with 15 new "flattops" launched by the Japanese.

The Navy lost five major carriers, or CVs (the "V" being simply an aeronautical designator), and six light or escort CVLs or CVEs, while destroying fifteen of Japan's. The enemy ended the war with only two afloat.

The hard core of the CV force was the war-born *Essex* class. As close to the naval equivalent of assembly-line men-of-war as technically possible, twenty-four of those 27,100-ton seaborne weapons on the grand scale were hurried into commission.

They stretched out to 885 feet (one-sixth of a mile) overall, with a 93-foot beam, making them not quite so large nor so graceful as the *Lexington-Saratoga* prewar class. Of the two, "Lady Lex" was lost at the Battle of the Coral Sea just five months following Pearl Harbor.

Also, the *Essex* carriers were little better than half the size of the *Midway* Class of 45,000 tons (including as well the *Franklin D. Roosevelt* and *Coral Sea*), which arrived too late to claim a slice of the victory. In turn, the *Midway* was something like half the size of the nuclear *Enterprise* and *Nimitz*. Of these two the former began sea duty about a quarter of a century after Pearl Harbor.

The *Essex* squadrons became the hard cutting edge, the dependable workhorses along the Navy's sea road to Tokyo. Without the sting from their massive flocks of planes—one hundred to a carrier—VJ Day most surely would have been postponed. And there are those who still insist that their continued application would have made the use of the A-bombs unnecessary.

They were something else, too—the wings of tomorrow in carrier design and concept for mid-twentieth-century warfare. Their triumphs as well as punishments provided architectural inspiration for the Navy's coming squadrons of airfields afloat. They assured the place of the carrier in naval operations of the future.

Not one of the proud *Essex* class was lost in combat. This was a tribute to both their maneuverability and damage control and the skill and courage of the crews. In the dying months of the war, however, that record was challenged. One nearly did not make it home. It happens to be the subject of this chronicle.

ACKNOWLEDGMENTS

The author wishes to thank especially for their assistance in the preparation of this book these survivors of the *Franklin*: Kermit Clingerman, Poland, Ohio; Carroll K. "Budd" Faught of Washington, D.C., an official of the U.S. Government who is still a pilot in spite of an artificial limb; S. Aaron Gill of Alexandria, Virginia; Jack Grove, Frederick, Maryland; Capt. Richard E. Jortberg, Washington, D.C.; MacGregor Kilpatrick, Branford, Connecticut; John O'Donovan, Norwalk, Connecticut; and Henry K. Willard, Washington, D.C., the seaman who ultimately became vice-president of one of his city's largest banks.

He also acknowledges the splendid help of David Berger, Philadelphia, Pennsylvania; Adm. Gerald F. Bogan, USN (ret.), La Jolla, California; Capt. Charles H. Carr, USN (ret.), Long Beach California; George W. Cheney, Jr., Hartford, Connecticut; Zell Davis, Jr., West Palm Beach, Florida; the late Vice Adm. Ralph Davison, USN, Pensacola, Florida, who died before this book was completed; Msgr. William Farrell of the (Catholic) Archdiocese of Washington, D.C., the Yeoman "Bill" Farrell referred to by Clingerman and believed as well to be the yeoman encountered by Jack Grove; Chief Bill Fowler, Glen Burnie, Maryland; Dr. James L. Fuelling, Jr., Marion, Indiana; Richard Fulfarr, East Meadow, New York, secretary of the *Franklin* Committee; Cdr. Donard Gary, USN (ret.), Garden Grove, California; Rear Adm. Leslie Gehres, USN (ret.), San Diego, California; Joseph Gruttadauria, Rochester, New York; Capt. Robert S. Hayes, Washington, D.C.; Capt. William B. Hayler, USN (ret.), Vallejo, California; Richard H. Johnston,

Homewood, Illinois; Joseph F. Lafferty, Floral Park, New York; Santo Lo Furno, Rochester, New York; Rear Adm. William R. McKinney, Arlington, Virginia; Adm. James S. Russell, USN (ret.), Tacoma, Washington; Dr. Sam Sherman, Mt. Zion Hospital and Medical Center, San Francisco, California; Norman Titus, Indianapolis, Indiana; Roy G. Treadaway, San Angelo, Texas; E. Robert Wassman, Larchmont, New York; and Hoyt Williams, Decatur, Georgia.

A number of people not connected directly with the *Franklin* also provided great aid in the research of the book. They include Vice Adm. E. M. Hooper, Director of Naval History, and Dean Allard of his staff, who dug into their archives for valuable after-action reports, especially those of Gehres, his executive officer, Joe Taylor (now deceased), Thomas J. Greene, the engineering officer, and Steve Jurika, the navigating officer.

The author as well wishes to acknowledge the aid of Alexander Crosby Brown of the Newport News (Virginia) *Times-Herald*, author, Navy man, and authority on all things nautical; and of the public relations department of Holy Cross College, Worcester, Massachusetts, where the late Chaplain O'Callahan taught.

To: Commander-in-Chief U.S. Fleet
Ref. (a) Pac Flt Conf. ltr 1CL-45

1. On 14 March, 1945, Fast Carrier Task Force 58 sortied from Ulithi for combat operations against Japan. The Task Force proceeded north to launch sustained strikes on targets on the island of Kyushu. The element of surprise was not attained, enemy aircraft being active in the vicinity of the force from about 2200, 17 March on. Attacks, mostly single, were made on the various Task Groups at frequent intervals and many planes were shot down by the CAP [combat air patrol] and AA [anti-aircraft] fire. On 18 March strikes were launched as scheduled.

2. During the night of 18-19 March the Task Force retired to the southeast. On the morning of 19 March TF 58 returned northward to launch strikes against naval and merchant shipping in the Inland Sea. The Task Force met with heavy Japanese air opposition. . . .

THE
FRANKLIN
COMES
HOME

1

NO ELEMENT
OF SURPRISE

The USS *Franklin*, better known on naval lists as CV-13 and to her people as "Big Ben," celebrated New Year's Day, 1945, perched drably on keel blocks in the Bremerton Shipyard, Puget Sound, Washington.* A cold drizzle all too typical of winter along the North Pacific coast mattered little to her complement of some 2,500 officers and enlisted men. Most were home on holiday leave since the carrier could not provide for more than a skeleton crew while in drydock.

In fact, she evoked memories of her launching in October, 1943, at Newport News, Virginia, when one of the first seamen assigned had observed:

> I stood on the dock and set down my seabag. Then I pushed back my hat on my head and just looked. There she was—my ship, no name, no planes, no bridge, no guns. Just a great big hull—the biggest hunk of steel I'd ever seen in my life. Looked like a floating table top. On that I was going off to fight a war.

* She was named for the Battle of Franklin, Tennessee, in the Civil War rather than for Benjamin Franklin.

In operation only six months by late autumn, 1944, the *Franklin* was already battle-scarred. She had assuredly sailed off "to fight a war." This was why she was being patched up, repainted, and generally refurbished for her next round with the foe.

The carrier had made her battle debut in July, 1944, during strikes against the Bonins, a meager land chain only 600 miles from Japan's southeast flanks; next, she went against a more formidable bastion to the south, the Marianas, which were astride the eastern sea extremity of the Philippines.

During that summer the *Franklin*'s planes were almost continuously aloft. They destroyed enemy shipping, seaplane bases, radio transmitters, and other island installations as well as "numerous" aircraft stamped with the emblem of the Rising Sun. Some pilots inevitably did not return; a few were the victims of accidents, such as crash landings, destroyed as surely as if enemy AA fire had knocked them from the darkened skies.

Tokyo Rose had already sunk Big Ben four times.

Not until mid-October did the carrier make use of her main battery of twelve 5-inch-38 guns and secondary nests of 3-inchers, 40 mm's, and 20 mm's. Covering the operations against Leyte in the Philippines, Big Ben miraculously escaped several aerial torpedoes, although one Japanese plane crashed onto her spacious deck, then slid off to starboard into the sea before exploding. Those who remarked on such things noted that it was Friday the 13th. Air Group 13 was in action and the *Franklin* herself was, of course, the CV-13.

The next day, the 14th, still during the Battle of Leyte Gulf, a bomb smashed onto the deck-edge plane elevator, killing three crewmen and wounding twenty-two. It was the first anniversary of the *Franklin*'s christening.

The carrier buried her dead, hospitalized her injured in sick bay, and slugged on. Her planes during the ensuing five days destroyed ships in Manila Bay, a floating dry dock, and bagged eleven enemy aircraft. The task group of which she was a part sank four enemy carriers, virtually eliminating this class of capital ship from the Imperial Navy.

Notwithstanding her casualties, the *Franklin* still appeared to her crew to be "a very lucky ship." This seeming beneficence of fate ran out, however, on October 30, 1944, off Samar in the Philippines.

"I saw it coming far out on the horizon," recalled Ens. Richard E. Jortberg of Portland, Maine, whose Naval Academy Class of 1945 had graduated a year early. "The speck looked at first as though it were eighty miles away, winging in on a dead-eye course. We knew at once what it was—Kamikaze!"

Actually, the "speck" turned out to be not one but six determined suicide planes. The first missed. The second hit another carrier, the *Belleau Wood*.

Watching these Kamikazes was Jack Grove, an eighteen-year-old aviation ordnance man from Frederick, Maryland, who had been with the *Franklin* since her commissioning. Suddenly, he was seized with the feeling that he was quite alone. His shipmates, with good reason, were racing from the flight deck to seek cover.

When he saw the wing lights of one aircraft—a single-engined Zeke—and its guns seemingly strafing, Jack knew it was time to run. He pressed himself against the rungs of a ladder leading up to a quad 40-mm mount "so hard it seemed I was trying to get into the iron!"

Time ran out. The Zeke hit the deck "with a crunching sound and an explosion," a little more than twenty feet away. When he smelled something burning, Jack looked and discovered that it was his life jacket.

Aside from those burns, however, Jack Grove was lucky. Fifty-six others on the *Franklin* died in the suicide plunge, sixty more were wounded.

The damage itself—centering around a fifty-foot hole in the flight deck—was temporarily repaired with emergency plates carried for such a purpose and quickly riveted on. Planes were landing again in little more than twenty minutes.

The pilot of the Kamikaze, who was instantly killed, was not badly disfigured. A letter and mementoes from home were found intact in his pockets. Indeed, from such relics, naval intelligence had gleaned much information about this strange *"Banzai!"* breed of aviator who died so obediently for his Emperor. For example, not only did he aim specifically for the carrier elevators, but he knew from flag hoists and positioning in the task force which was the flag carrier, bearing the admiral.

Patched up, the *Franklin* nonetheless had to return to Bremerton for permanent repairs. She hove to in Puget Sound just a few days too late for Thanksgiving but in ample time for the Christmas holidays.

The towering man-of-war languished through the festive season, a hurt giant licking its wounds. Ashore, there were parties aplenty, arranged by all sorts of citizen groups in the greater Portland area. It wasn't easy for a sailor to pay for anything out of his own wallet.

The *Franklin*'s "old man" since November 2 had been Leslie Edward Gehres, a six-foot-four barrel-chested veteran of the First World War, tough and "reg" in the salty, crusty tradition of John Paul Jones, Perry, Decatur, Farragut, all of the Navy's hell-for-canvas no-nonsense immortals. The massive forty-nine-year-old aviator had wanted this combat assignment so badly that he had voluntarily stepped down to captain from his new commodore's rank. The brass was not even tarnished on his wide stripe of rank.

Gehres, who grew up in Rochester, New York, was first an enlisted "swabbie," then a Reserve ensign in 1918. He cut his sea teeth on several vessels, including the old battleship

Massachusetts. In 1927 he won his wings, then flew for a decade as a member of the acrobatic team, the "High Hat" squadron. The group performed at air races and won successive awards including the best for acrobatics at the All-American Air Maneuvers in Miami in 1936.

He flew from most of the carriers commissioned during the 1930s, including the *Lexington.* He took Fleet Air Wing Four—composed of two-engined PBY Catalinas—to Dutch Harbor, Alaska, in May, 1942, about ten days before the Japs struck. These slow flying-boats spearheaded that remote area's indifferent aerial defenses against the aggressor at a price of four lost. This was a diversionary blow to mask the major Battle of Midway.

Gehres, with slightly better aircraft, led bombing raids against the Japanese-held Kuriles and also aided in driving the enemy out of their tenuous footholds in the Aleutians.

Big Les Gehres became a legend in this northerly outpost, both for his effectiveness as a pilot and a fighting man and for his personality traits. Once he had a cow flown in to supply him with fresh milk only to find that "Bossie" had dried up. He was more successful with a shipment of bricks for a fireplace. Something of a dandy, he was never seen without well-polished fingernails.

Pilots cursed him for sending them into Alaska's fearsome weather—"Unflyable!" they railed. He did nothing for their morale when he announced at a briefing, "I don't expect to see hardly any of you guys alive before we're through!"

In 1943 Gehres became the Navy's first aviation commodore. He brought with him to the *Franklin* an athletic coach's *esprit de corps* and heartiness combined with an overriding zeal to mold all aboard into at least the stereotype of a sailor. This sparked acutely mixed reactions from the pilots, who never really thought of themselves as part of a ship's company. They fumed, for example, at demands that they stand "conning" watches on the bridge. "Go get 'em!"

the big commanding officer would sometimes exhort in un-constrained enthusiasm as a flight zoomed off. Then he would smash his ham fists together and stride about excit-edly.

While Gehres chafed at inaction, shambling Bunyan-like among the workmen, repairs and "mods" (modifications) at Bremerton continued. Modifications were introduced when-ever a warship was docked for an appreciable time. They ranged all the way from a new anchor windlass to replace-ment nests of rapid-firing guns. The mods also included al-terations as seemingly inconsequential or diminutive as different tubes in a radio transmitter or stronger "dogging" bolts for a hatch.

The major modification on the *Franklin* was the relocation of the Combat Information Center (CIC) from the "is-land," or main bridge-navigation superstructure, to the for-ward part of the gallery deck. The latter was above and alongside the spacious hangar deck.

CIC, with its clusters of radars, computers, plot and maneuvering boards, gyroscopic compass repeaters, gauges, headsets, phones, and tubes, was the brain of a fighting ship. At general quarters it was manned by approximately twelve officers and thirty men, who coordinated fire control and, if necessary, vital information as to internal damage relayed from the Central Damage Control Station, farther below.

All in all, the relocation seemed logical. The space had been cramped on the island. In addition, the latter position was more vulnerable to attacking aircraft.

Then—great day!—Big Ben was afloat again in the ship-yard, off her blocks and a back-to-normal port routine was reestablished—morning "masts" for stragglers and other offenders, sick calls, morning colors, "Now hear this!", "Sweepers lay down . . . !"—all against the gray, redolent backdrop of a hammering, whistling shipyard.

In an unusual expression of gratitude, Captain Gehres

faced the ship's public address system to thank the yard crew for the "excellence" of the work. On January 25 the *Franklin* rode at anchor in Sinclair Inlet, a taut ship once more, in Gehres' nautical nomenclature.

A week later she upped anchor, showing her broad, square stern to the mists of Juan de Fuca Strait and the snowy peaks of the Olympic Mountains behind Cape Flattery as she butted her blunt prow and landing deck overhang out into rougher seas en route south to the Alameda Naval Air Station. There she would pick up Air Group No. 5. The pilots, mechanics, administrative crewmen, and officers would swell Big Ben's population to approximately 3,200.

Aside from the hard core of some 600 war-wise petty officers and chief petty officers, many aboard were green reservists or enlistees who had never before been to sea. Yet any who might have been prone to homesickness had scant time to indulge such a tendency in the accelerating activity of a capital ship standing out to the broad Pacific Ocean.

Among the diversions was a large and enthusiastic ship's band led by a well-known recording musician, Horace "Saxie" Dowell, a North Carolinian whose compositions, "Playmate" and "Three Little Fishies," were familiar to the dance, radio, and platter set.

On February 13 Big Ben moored abeam of Ford Island in Pearl Harbor. The great naval anchorage still showed the scars of December 7, 1941. Sunken wreckage of the battleships *Arizona* and *Utah* continued to thwart salvage crews, although other warships of the Pacific Fleet had been raised. Most of them were back in operation, and a few had been present at the invasion of Normandy the past June.

For the remainder of February and into the first week of March the *Franklin* steamed in maneuvers off the Hawaiian Islands, affording practice for her aerial squadrons. Like the changing guest list of a hotel, some officers and men arrived for duty, others signed off.

One reporting aboard was Capt. Arnold J. "Izzy" (variously, "Buster") Isbell, of Logan, Iowa, who had distinguished himself as a pilot as well as commanding officer of the escort carrier *Card*. She was mother eagle to one of several hunter-killer groups that were exacting a toll of U-boats in the Atlantic. The 1921 Annapolis graduate was a passenger this time, en route to his new command, the *Yorktown*. She, too, belonged to the *Essex* class, being named for the ship lost after the Battle of Midway.

Another arrival was a bespectacled former mathematics professor at Holy Cross College in Worcester, Massachusetts, Joseph Timothy O'Callahan. The forty-year-old chaplain with a face that appeared to some people as that of "a perennial altar boy" came from a large Roxbury, Massachusetts, family. A sister, Rose Marie, who was a Maryknoll nun, had been imprisoned by the Japanese in the Philippines.

Father O'Callahan's undergraduate days had been a mosaic of athletics (accenting track), dramatics, poetry, philosophy, and writing, both scholastic and religious. Exceptionally devout even by the Jesuit yardstick, he laced his speech, themes, and correspondence with references to the Deity and the saints. Withal, he managed to bridge the natural gap between a cleric and the laity through a natural ability to identify and communicate with his shipmates. Aboard the carrier *Ranger* in European waters, O'Callahan was frequently alluded to by members of the Jewish faith with affectionate incongruity as "Rabbi Tim." Pilots called him simply "Joe."

During his short three months' shore duty at Pearl Harbor the popular chaplain yearned to return to sea. Much of his impatience was occasioned by the fervent but dim hope that he might be able to reach the Philippines, now partially liberated, to ascertain if his sister still survived.

With O'Callahan came "gear" in such volume as to suggest an admiral's ownership. As several large crates were hoisted aboard, he admonished, "Careful, lad, many religious books there!" Then, with a wink to an officer next to him, he added in a whisper, "Those books might break." Inside were bottles of Scotch, bourbon, and beer, a testament to the chaplain's worldly propensities. He knew there were times when prayer alone might not be quite sufficient. But what he did not know was how soon.

What the chaplain or anyone else toted aboard, however, was minuscle compared to the mountains of supplies being transferred from the dock--when the carrier was beside a dock—to the quarter deck. Since the structural eccentricities of such a vessel make a quarter deck (normally in the upper stern section) more a state of mind than an actuality, the hangar deck had to double in that role.

Day by day the ridges of potatoes, cabbage, flour and sugar sacks, frozen sides of beef and pork, plus crates of everything from eggs to ketchup and even small- and large-caliber ammunition lowered as they moved up and onto the hangar deck. There they were trundled off by sweating work details to many storage areas of the *Franklin*, including frozen food lockers. The "heavy stuff" (bombs) was transferred from lighters when at anchorage in designated "explosive" areas.

There was bedlam of a sort on the quarter deck, but nonetheless authority. The loading went on in such volume as to suggest a round-the-world cruise of decidedly martial flavor.

Ultimately, however, storage space as well as accommodations was exhausted. None of the 3,226 souls aboard—not even the many officers of the quarter deck who had supervised the procedure—could count exactly how many tons of cargo had been loaded. There were so many bombs and rockets, for example, that they were stored in the heads, or toilets, all over the carrier.

Maneuvers, too, were completed. Diamond Head dropped

astern as the *Franklin* steamed into the Pacific under an all-too-familiar blackout.

Gehres announced over the PA system, "We are sailing northward, a part of Task Force Fifty-eight, bound to strike the Home Islands of the Japanese Empire for the first time!" He savored his role as conveyor of tidings like a newscaster dramatically interrupting a broadcast to "bring you this bulletin!" Leslie Gehres sniffed battle with the ill-suppressed and swashbuckling excitement of a Farragut. Some suggested he was the nautical equivalent of war-loving "Blood and Guts" Patton.

On March 15 the carrier hove to off Ulithi Lagoon in the West Caroline Islands. This impressive staging area was no sanctuary, though, since the carrier *Randolph* had been hit while at anchor there by a Kamikaze.

True to her master's announcement, the *Franklin* rendezvoused with the mightiest striking unit in the history of naval warfare: Task Force 58. It was so large that it had to be subdivided into components: .1, .2, .3, and .4. Its approximately one hundred surface vessels were committed to the protection of at least fifteen, sometimes sixteen, fast carriers, predominantly of the *Essex* class.

Task Force 58, a designation interchangeable with the former 38—mainly to confound the enemy—was under command of Adm. Marc A. Mitscher, Class of 1910, pioneer naval aviator who piloted the NC-1, one of the "Nancies," in the attempt to fly the Atlantic in 1919. "Pete" Mitscher, who also helped develop the catapult, was lean and quiet, with the perpetual squint of pilot and seafarer. He flew his four-star flag from the carrier *Bunker Hill*.

The commander of the Third Fleet, of which Task Force 58 was the mightiest component, was Adm. William F. Halsey. "Bull" Halsey, Annapolis 1904, of average height and stocky, had earned his niche along with Gen. Douglas MacArthur in the deepest apprehensions of the Japanese. He was far more flamboyant than the executivelike Mitscher, better copy for the correspondents. The two ranking admirals nonetheless thought alike tactically and formed an apparently flawless team.

An old friend returned to the *Franklin* at Ulithi. Adm. Ralph E. Davison from St. Louis, forty-nine years old, who had previously hoisted his task group flag on the carrier's lofty yards, led group No. 58.2, Carrier Division 2. With a personality similar to Mitscher's, unassuming almost to reticence, Davison, Naval Academy, 1916, was again a familiar boyish-faced figure on the flag bridge. Binoculars slung around his neck, he once more observed the changing patterns of the many gray warships under his aegis. Davison was considered brilliant by his staffers. He was strict but he was also considerate of the feelings and prerogatives of those under his command.

He was worried about this approaching sortie, mindful of the loss of the light carrier *Princeton* at Leyte Gulf and the intensification of Kamikaze attacks. With Mitscher and his staff, he worked out a procedure for a carrier hit and afire. Carrier commanders were instructed to induce a heel to port by putting the ship in a tight turn to starboard initially, in order to spill fuel from ruptured aircraft tanks and water from hangar sprinkling and flight deck hoses over the port side away from conflagration control stations and flight deck repair lockers.

The two closest cruisers were to go to the wounded carrier's assistance, one to help in fighting fires from alongside and one to be prepared to tow. Destroyers—of which the great number of twenty-four formed a circular screen around each task group—were to maintain their role as submarine and aircraft screen except when summoned for specific rescue operations.

Mitscher approved the plan, which was written into the task group operation order.

This time, Admiral Davison was accompanied by a classmate, Adm. General F. "Gerry" Bogan. He was due to relieve
Davison in a few weeks, or as soon as the present operation
was completed.

On Saturday and Sunday, March 17 and 18, the task force
was spread over 50 miles of darkening Pacific Ocean, nearing the coasts of Shikoku, one of the Home Islands, and slim
Kyushu, 200 miles long, the southernmost of the Japanese
group. This was "Nippon's private lake." Here, winter remained, even as it did off much of the American East Coast.
Seas were rough and cold. A steady west wind blew out of
overcast skies.

Notwithstanding months of incessant bombardment from
sea and air, even from bold submarines which surfaced inside bays to blast with their deck guns oil tanks, warehouses,
and all manner of targets including trains, still more destruction was to be wrought. Hangars, airfields, aircraft, and
harbor traffic persisted, and these were among the objectives. Perhaps the prime mission of the task force was to
neutralize Japanese airpower in order to prepare for an invasion.

By Saturday evening the *Franklin*, pounding up from the
south, was readying her planes for strikes against Kogo-
shima, on Kyushu, and other targets on Osumi Island to the
south. Eighteen enemy planes were shot down by Air Group
5, while others were exploded on the ground, together with
their hangars and small boats tied up along the inlets.

Some of the Japanese planes were destroyed within sight
of the task force. One plunged vertically at the carrier *Intrepid*, missing by a few feet. Witnesses said the attacker
had started his dive from five miles up.

The combat air patrol roared through the clouds, searching for the foe. The weather was unfavorable. Sometimes a
plane was pursued wildly for miles only to turn out to be
friendly.

The *Franklin* lost four Corsair fighter-bombers that day. One pilot was rescued, however, by a "lifeguard" submarine offshore. Another was lost in a photo finish between an oncoming rescue submarine and two armed Japanese sampans. The latter, Lt. J. Pierpont Stodd III of Portland, Oregon, waved from his yellow rubber raft to circling carrier pilots. They strafed the sampans—to no avail. Stodd was captured by the enemy.

The navigator's plot board high atop the ship's island showed, in spite of zigzagging and course changes—even reversals of direction as she doubled back over her own wake—progressive hauling up nearer to the foe's islands. Drifting mines whispered of the proximity and menace of the channels into Japanese ports. Gunners popped most of these with rapid-firing multiple mounts. The target practice was welcome.

Electrically "degaussed," as were all Navy ships, the *Franklin* was relatively impervious to magnetic mines. Fleet minesweepers were charged with clearing more intricate and diabolic types such as the acoustic, which were exploded by propeller sound (sometimes of the third, or even twelfth, vessel to pass over them), or those moored at varying depths beneath the surface, set to detonate on contact.

Fleet submarines, scouting far ahead of the task force, with Kyushu's shoreline often framed in their periscopes, were on the alert for the few remaining enemy undersea boats as well as for attacking aircraft. The Navy submarines also bore the prime mission of rescuing downed American pilots, as they had already done this day.

Saturday night, Japanese aviators announced their arrival over the perimeters of the task force through blossoming flares. Their white-yellow brilliance, intruding into the protective mantle of darkness to silhouette the sea of warships, was at once startling and weirdly beautiful.

Antiaircraft fire from picket destroyers stabbed back. On

the heavy cruiser *Santa Fe* the quartermaster, possibly with tongue in cheek, wrote in his log, "The element of surprise was not attained."

"Bogies," or unidentified aircraft "blipping" electronically across radar screens, could turn out to be friendly. This possibility imposed an ultimate test on the gunners' self-control. Pilots touched down on their flight decks swearing at the flak from the fleet through which they had been forced to plow in these crowded skies.

And so Task Force 58 bore in. Its role in these climactic days of World War II complemented that of America's soldiers, sailors, and airmen on the many far-flung arenas of operation. B-29 four-engined bombers had just set much of Tokyo and Nagoya aflame. Returning in his Superfortress from a mission over Nagoya, a pilot, Col. Carl R. Storrie of Denton, Texas, summed up bluntly, "We burned hell out of it!"

All Japanese resistance had just ceased on hotly contested Iwo Jima. General MacArthur had invaded Panay in the central Philippines, the last of the island group to be recaptured.

The Asiatic enemy was edgy. Wire service reports quoted Tokyo as saying that an American fleet had set out from the Marianas "for an unknown destination." The news syndicates added, on their own, "There was nothing from American sources to substantiate these rumors."

Two thousand planes—bombers and fighters—had darkened the skies in one of the mightiest raids over badly ravaged Berlin.

The First Army poured across the Rhine's Remagen Bridge in significant numbers prior to the span's collapse on the 17th. The Seventh Army was deep in the Saar, while General Patton's Third Army was across the strategic Moselle.

The Russians were fighting in the east like blooded panthers, closing in for the kill. Clearing out German pockets in Upper Silesia, Soviet armies had swept twenty-five miles through East Prussia, in a three-day offensive. The Baltic coast was near.

Winston Churchill was confidently predicting the war's end by late summer, or possibly even sooner.

All in all, it appeared likely enough.

2

"THERE'S ONE COMING
TOWARDS YOU!"

At dawn on Sunday, March 18, the *Franklin* was steaming at
17 knots due east of the northernmost Ryukyus and about
135 miles southeast of the tip of Kyushu. At 0605, by the
navigator's log, bogies, or "bandits," were reported to be
"closing fast."

Course was changed. Additional planes were launched.

At 0740 the speed was raised to twenty-four knots, representing 182 RPMs (revolutions per minute) of the carrier's
enormous quadruple propellers.

The *Intrepid*, a flattop in another task group, came under
sudden attack by a single enemy plane. The aircraft was as
quickly knocked out of the skies.

The church flag was now unfurled on the forward trucks
above the Stars and Stripes. O'Callahan and his Protestant
counterpart, Grimes "Gats" Gatlin, a Texan, were holding
their services on separate sections of the auditoriumlike hangar deck. In its same oily vastness motion pictures were
shown on quieter nights. Many present would recall that
O'Callahan, perhaps prophetically, granted "general absolution" to all Catholics assembled.

Shortly after noon one of the *Franklin's* planes staggered in for a crash landing. There were no injuries.

"We took especial satisfaction in bombing Kagoshima," recalled Lt. Carroll K. "Budd" Faught, of the only Marine squadron aboard. "For it was here the Japs practiced for Pearl Harbor, since the configuration of the bay was similar."

Faught, from Wyoming, was a member of a famous squadron—VMF-214—since it had been commanded by the ace, Maj. Gregory "Pappy" Boyington, until his capture at Rabaul by the enemy. The unit, known to its members as the "Black Sheep" squadron, had recently completed practice in the Mohave Desert with new 5-inch "Holy Moses" rockets.

The squadron and especially the stocky, dark-haired Budd Faught were well known to Gehres. On one occasion, exercising a fighter pilot's privilege for a clear track to his plane after "Scramble!" was sounded, Faught was tearing along a passageway, shouting, as customary, "Gangway for a fighter pilot!" Suddenly he crashed headlong into the ample midriff of a very large man: none other than the captain of the *Franklin.*

Another time, he was called to the bridge when Gehres did not like his landing. The commander had some reason for concern since the plane's undercarriage had been slightly damaged. Gehres began the interview in a brusque fashion, his deep frown a testament to his irritation, then made a sudden switch and invited Faught to dinner, afterwards taking him on a tour of the engine room. "I guess he wanted to show me how hard his crew worked," Faught averred.

The routine of Sunday at sea passed. The customary Sabbath feast was scantier, surely more rushed than normal. There was almost no time for seated meals. In fact, only one meal was provided that day "despite every effort to feed the crew," according to Gehres.

There were, however, "Burny's pies" aplenty, as indeed there had been ever since Bob Burny had come aboard. The heir to the large Burny Brothers Bakery of Chicago, young Burny, a ship's cook, had brought all of his father's celebrated pie recipes with him. Working under the disadvantages of shipboard cooking, especially prior baking, Burny did his best to reproduce at least a taste of his father's pies and hot breads in the Western Pacific.

Late in the afternoon, pilots who weren't on night patrol were likely to make use of their private stores of liquor. For one, Budd Faught had purchased two cases of Philadelphia-brand bourbon in Pearl Harbor, which was conveniently augmenting Father O'Callahan's already ample stores. The two men had quarters facing across a passageway. "The padre and I used to have wonderful talks of an evening," Faught observes.

At sunset the landing signal officers with their lighted paddle wands waved in the last planes. The night would be short enough for the pilots. In the morning many would take off for attacks on the big, active ports of Kure and Kobe, astride the shores of Honshu, the main Home Island. Kobe was perhaps Japan's most important naval base. In order to assure "ample return range" even with maximum bomb load, the carrier had to maneuver within sixty miles of the Kyushu coast by dawn. This would bring her closer than any flattop had ventured to the Japanese mainland and her "Inland Sea."

Darkness finally was complete, but there was no rest for the ship's crew. Shortly after midnight the *Franklin* went on defense against torpedoes and never fully secured from that condition of readiness.

The Captain would write:

> The night of the 18th was one of recurrent alarms, the
> ship being at torpedo defense stations a large part of

the night. Many bogeys showed on the screen, considerable firing took place in the task groups on either side of Task Group 58.2. Night fighters were active. The rearming and maintenance crews of the Air Department worked steadily all night long.

The quartermaster's log tallied twelve separate general quarters (GQ), a piercing, never-to-be-forgotten alarm on the bugle through the carrier's amplifier system. Crewmen were just dozing off after the last one when shortly after 3 A.M. the strident notes again sent them tumbling to gun "tubs," fire stations, critically placed hatches, and other GQ posts: "All hands to general quarters! Man all battle stations . . . on the double!"

A lone Japanese scout plane was dropping flares over the task force. The battleship *North Carolina* blanketed the intruder with bursts as other ships, including the *Franklin*, added to the barrage. Night fighters droned up from the decks of several carriers.

Gehres, in his darkened glass-enclosed bridge, would observe laconically that the counterfire had produced "no visible results."

Radio chatter among the ships during this disturbed night was filled with messages such as: "Hold fire! Friendly chicken passing from north!" Or, "Batteries released."

There was a continuing humdrum indicating course and speed changes, and, towards morning, zigzags "according to Plan 6" or another pattern.

Chaplain O'Callahan performed needed morale services during the night by visiting the men at their stations and sometimes going on the intercom to volunteer progress reports. A noncombatant with no battle station, the priest felt he had to move his "weary old bones" about the carrier from area to area, treading cautiously in unfamiliar darkened surroundings, ducking his head, and holding a hand before his face to protect his glasses. By keeping in touch with the bridge or CIC, O'Callahan was able to keep up to date on, for example, enemy planes shot down by Navy "night chickens."

Combat conditions were a strain on all the ship's company, from mess boys and "ordinaries" (seamen) on up to the eyries of command. Nowhere was the tension more acute than in CIC. For most of Saturday and Sunday virtually the whole watch had worked without relief, straining eyes against the subdued brilliance of radar screens, engulfed in a miasma of cigarette smoke.

George Cheney, still a fighter director, would recall:

> By midnight, night fighter action finally let up a bit. It seemed that most of us who had been on station in CIC the better part of these two days could catch a few hours' sleep. We drew lots to see who should stay beyond midnight for the midwatch.

Cheney, another officer, and a dozen radarmen lost and had to stay on till the morning watch. Cheney was relieved at 4 A.M., when he went below—but only for three hours.

In sick bay, also known as the hospital ward aft on No. 1 deck, the night had become quiet with the merciful death of a young seaman poisoned by drinking "bug juice," or torpedo fluid. He had been crying out in agony despite the ministrations of youthful Lt. Cdr. George W. "Bill" Fox of Milwaukee and his seven pharmacist mates.

Fox was a skillful surgeon. He had snatched back many flickering lives at sea with internal as well as brain surgery. Sick or wounded sailors had faith that no matter what happened to them "Doc" Fox would pull them through. But no one could save a man who had drunk the wood alcohol compound in torpedo propellants, even though it had been strained through bread—an illusion that had already caused the deaths of many Navy men.

Now, there were only eleven patients in sick bay, including Joseph Gruttadauria of Rochester, New York, an aviation ordnanceman with the air group. Joe, in for a bad reaction he had experienced from immunization shots, had, like the others, been kept awake for hours by the dying youth's screams.

The night was still black and foreboding at 5:30 A.M., about a half-hour before dawn, when the *Franklin* commenced activities for Monday the 19th, designated in Task Force 58 code as "Lucky Plus One" day. At that time, the ship came into the wind, on a northeast course. One by one, thirty Corsairs, fatly pregnant with a new-type rocket, the "Tiny Tim," to be fired against the naval base at Kure, thundered off the flight deck. Tiny Tims were actually twelve inches in diameter and so heavy they had to be wheeled about on sturdy dollies.

By 6 A.M. the last bluish exhaust flame had vanished into the west where the closest parcel of enemy land, Kyushu, was now some fifty-five miles distant—two hours' steaming.

The gunnery officer, Lt. Cdr. William R. McKinney, Class of 1940, relayed orders from Admiral Davison, the task force commander, to set Condition 3, a watch scaled down in numbers of gunners at their stations since the radar screen appeared clear of bogies.

The carrier was, however, almost completely "buttoned up" in Condition Z, or "Zebra." The majority of the hatches were closed in a battle-zone state of readiness designed to prevent both flooding and the spread of fires. A number of hatches in the hangar deck, however, *were* open for the hoisting of stores from below.

The new "condition" meant that general quarters had again been secured, something that seemed inconceivable to at least one man aboard: Yeoman 2c Joseph Lafferty of Brooklyn, one of the first to report aboard the ship at Newport News. Though he was one of the captain's yeomen, his battle station was six decks deep in the carrier, in damage control, where he was a "talker."

Joe Lafferty observed to the man next to him that the captain "must be out of his mind." Through his earphones, as picked up from above-decks portions of the far-reaching intercom system, Lafferty could still hear guns firing in the distance. He questioned the order and found it was correct. He was supposed to quit his station and "chow down"— breakfast.

This was all right with Lafferty, who did not like anything about that deeply situated battle station, especially the headset under his helmet which hurt his ears. Like most sailors he preferred to be where he could see what was going on. So he started up the ladders

> and through holes big enough for a thin man. I climbed to the second deck where the captain's office was located, entering the office with my helmet on. It was crowded with other yeoman and an enlisted man who had come out of Chief of Naval Personnel, Hawaii.
>
> His duty was to write human interest stories about the crew. He had written a story about me and about Brooklyn and was now commenting, "It was great standing on the bridge seeing the gun flashes and the enemy planes splashing into the dark Pacific."
>
> I turned as I took off my helmet and said, "Don't ever go topside without your helmet and Mae West on."

Others not remaining at their weapons answered the familiar, welcome call to chow down. Through the energy and devotion of the commissary department, a hot galley was kept sizzling around the clock. While relatively small groups off duty could be fed in scattered locations if need be, a line of hundreds of hungry men, plates in hand, wound about the planes and ammunition in the hangar deck, en route down to the galley on the next deck below. Much in evidence were the bulky Tiny Tims, resting heavily upon their carts waiting to be slung beneath the wings of aircraft.

In the senior wardroom Chaplain O'Callahan was kidding Tom Frasure, a steward's mate, about the cold "fried bread," a not uncommon Navy dish. It was generally tasteless no matter how earnestly disguised with butter and syrup.

Frasure parried in the same vein, "That ain't fried bread, that's French toast."

Then, recalling that this day was the Catholic feast of St. Joseph, the patron saint of a "kind" death, the priest grew quiet. He commenced eating the "fried bread."

In another eating space young Kermit Clingerman, a seaman first class from Berea, Ohio, was aware of a normal enough sound: "The clatter of trays, the general din of conversation and the overcrowded conditions of the messing compartments added to the monotony of a breakfast of powdered eggs, tomato juice, coffee, toast, and an apple."

Finished with his own "monotonous" breakfast, Dick Jortberg, who had been with the *Franklin* during her past year's baptisms, first walked through CIC on the gallery deck, a seeming sanctuary and the sensitive nerve center of the carrier.

Jortberg's own duties involved fire control—that is, the direction of the ship's antiaircraft fire. This morning he was junior officer of the deck in the pilot house on the bridge, or island, to starboard (right) of the flight deck and towering one hundred feet above the waterline. Down below, he could watch the next group of aircraft warming up, their propellers cutting the hazy predawn air. Pilots were already in their cockpits, mechanics and other crewmen waiting underneath the wings. Some held the ropes leading from the wheel chocks. Like the previous strike, these planes were also armed with Tiny Tim rockets.

On the fantail, at the hangar level, beneath the stern outjut of the flight deck, a burial party was completing a commitment ritual for the young enlisted man who had died during the night from drinking torpedo fluid. Officiating were Protestant Chaplain Gatlin and the executive officer, Cdr. Joseph Franklin Taylor from Danville, Illinois. A graduate of Annapolis, 1927, naval aviator and former test pilot, Joe was popular among his fellow officers. He had won Navy crosses for his actions at the Battle of the Coral Sea and at Guadalcanal.

As the bugle sounded the last mournful notes of taps, Taylor glanced at his wristwatch. It was just four minutes before 7 A.M., at which hour he knew the deckload strike was scheduled to take off.

There had been a delay, however, and possibly more time still would be required before the entire strike winged off. A patrol plane sniffing far out over Japan Bay had sighted what the pilot believed to be the battleship *Yamato*, of more than 73,000 tons, one of the largest in the world.

To attack her effectively meant that the contact bombs had to be changed to armor-piercing. This was now being done beside the planes.

Some pilots, in fact, such as Budd Faught, were in, beside, or en route to their planes when the bull horn advised them to return to the ready rooms for a new briefing. Swinging their helmets in their hands, they left the flight deck.

Taylor saluted the chaplain and "proceeded topside."

His successor in the all-important post of air-officer, Cdr. Henry Henderson Hale from Gary, Indiana, was now in effect the commanding officer of the carrier. His orders for the positioning of the *Franklin* or speeding or slowing it to aid in takeoffs must be unquestioningly and instantly obeyed. Hale was directing the lead plane of the morning's second strike into position on the runway.

The navigating officer, Philippine-born Cdr. Stephen Jurika, Class of 1933, walked out of the chart room where the red night light still glowed and blinked at the daylight. He advised the captain that the ship was only fifty-two miles due south of Point Ashizuri Saki on the southernmost tip of Shikoku. This, he observed with a frown, did seem close.

Onetime naval attaché in Tokyo, Jurika had a special reason for hating the enemy. His mother had been beheaded by the Japanese in Manila.

". . . Sea calm," he began to scribble notes for subsequent logging, "with a twelve-knot wind from about 060 true [the northeast] sky overcast with occasional breaks, lower scattered clouds at 1,500–2,500 feet. Horizontal visibility excellent."

In April 1942 Jurika had been intelligence officer aboard the *Enterprise* during Doolittle's Tokyo raid. Now, he was pounding in toward the Home Islands a second time, perhaps to avenge the murder of his mother.

It was just after daylight and "everything" was "ready," according to Lt. Fred Harris, the flight deck officer. The *Franklin's* speed was increased to twenty-four knots, or about thirty miles an hour. At three minutes before 7 A.M. the first plane of this strike was launched. It waddled into gray eastern skies, so familiar a sight that few not directly concerned with the operation even noticed.

Seconds before 7:05, as the seventh or, more likely, the eighth plane was revving up for takeoff, Dick Jortberg, still in the pilot house and standing between the helmsman and Steve Jurika, heard a scratchy message calling over the TBS, or short-range radio, from the carrier *Hancock*: "Enemy plane closing on you . . . one coming toward you!"

Motors were started on power mounts such as the 5-inch-38 twins and 40-mm quads. Those lighter, rapid-firing guns, including the 20-mm's, which had been in semireadiness, now were loaded. One of the gunnery director screens high on the island commenced searching with its fire-control radar.

At 7:06 CIC, which had been noting strangely clear radar

screens, reported, "Bogie orbiting on port beam, range about twelve miles."

A few seconds after 7:06, *Hancock* reemphasized, "Bogie closing you . . . !"

Firing Director One now picked up a "target" bearing about ten degrees, then lost it because of the confusion of planes being launched by the *Franklin* and other carriers. But there had been so many targets, so many bogies, they had become commonplace, especially so when measured against the crew's overriding weariness. What was one more bogie or bandit, more or less?

Then Jortberg listened to a call, possibly from a "talker" at a forward gun position: "We're going to get it!"

A pilot standing at the side of the flight deck, Lt. Arthur Schmagel of St. Louis, looked up and saw a swiftly approaching plane. Confidently, he "thought it was one of our boys trying to drop a message."

No guns were firing.

At that instant, logged variously as 7:07, 7:08, and 7:09 A.M., Jurika, "searching the sky overhead and also ahead for aircraft," saw two bombs "flash into my field of vision and hurtle down towards *Franklin*." He could not "see the enemy aircraft as such but glimpsed the flashing shadow as it swept past the island structure at about masthead height."

Split seconds too late, a 5-inch mount just forward of the superstructure spat its heavy shells at the retreating plane. Lookouts on the *Hancock* had already identified it as a "Judy," the effective aerial workhorse of the Japanese navy.

Still standing beside Steve Jurika, Jortberg did not witness even that much. All at once he was propelled up and up, until he hit the steel overhead that blanked his vision and set lights dazzling inside his head.

3

"I MIGHT AS WELL
HAVE SOME CASH."

Captain Gehres, also knocked off his feet, watched "great sheets of flame envelop the flight deck, the antiaircraft batteries and catwalks. The forward elevator—weighing thirty-two tons—rose in the air and then disappeared in a great column of flame and black smoke."

When John O'Donovan of Norwich, Connecticut, the quartermaster of the watch, saw "that elevator go up," he knew at once "we were in bad shape." In fact, as he attempted to log the attack in the QM's notebook, "it was a hell of a scrawl." He realized he was "badly scared" and his hand was shaking.

Still dazed, Gehres watched the column of flame and smoke "roll skyward" before it engulfed the bridge.

Capt. James S. Russell, Annapolis, 1926, Admiral Davison's chief of staff, stationed on the flag bridge below the carrier's pilot house, saw and heard it this way:

> Almost immediately there was a double crack of bomb hits. The ship lurched and a sheet of flame came out of the open door below us, which was of sufficient intensity to set fire to the outboard tires of the flight deck crash crane parked forward of the island.

Cdr. Robert Downes, the damage control officer, had just left his cabin. The concussion heaved him back, through the closed door and up against the outer bulkhead.

Executive Officer Joe Taylor, also close to the holocaust, was blown into the lifelines on the starboard side of the flight deck. Before him was a fiery panorama of chaos, caused by the first of what were believed to be two 500-pound bombs. They were placed, as the commanding officer would observe, like "an aviator's dream," since planes were caught gassed and bomb-laden; in total, 36,000 gallons of gasoline in the tanks and some 30 tons of bombs and rockets suspended from their racks.

Taylor watched helplessly as whirling propellers cut into the tails and fuselages of planes in front of and beside them. Others were tossed around by the blast. The pilot of one Helldiver, which had been flipped on its back in the act of taking off, was scrambling, upside down, out of the cockpit.

Ens. W. S. Richardson of Providence, Rhode Island, who had observed the enemy sweep over him after the bomb run, cut his engine and pushed back the canopy. It would have remained open had it not been for the cold morning air: ". . . I saw one big orange flash and a rocket whizzed about five feet over my head!" He crawled on his hands and knees as planes began blowing up around him "in big chunks," and finally made it to the island.

Radarman William C. Kallbrier of St. Louis, injured about his chest and legs in the badly battered radar plot, staggered through the smoke onto the deck to watch an engine blown from a plane go sailing into the sky so far "it seemed like it reached the horizon."

Flames had spread over five bombers, fourteen torpedo planes, and twelve fighters, armed or partly armed, on the flight and hangar decks. Other pilots and aviation or electronics personnel not so fortunate stumbled head-on into the propellers.

Those pilots who had left the deck were far luckier. In fact, one caught the Judy in his sights and shot it into the sea. Doubt would remain, nonetheless, as to whether the credit should go to Cdr. Erwin Parker of San Francisco, Air Group 5 CO, or one of his pilots.

Now Taylor headed aft, groping through the smoke. He lowered himself by a hand line onto one of the 40-mm gun sponsons (projecting platforms), climbed up onto a catwalk, and from there crawled through an opened port into the island.

He found "the smoke and flame . . . terrific. I started in every direction trying to get in the clear and orient myself." This he was unable to do. He soon found that he was back where he had started from, having gone in a nearly complete circle.

Below, Alvin S. McCoy of the Kansas City *Star*, representing the Combined American Press, had been waiting for his breakfast in the warrant officers' wardroom when he heard a "dull clanging explosion like the bedlam of a thousand boiler factories. The carrier shuddered. No one moved. 'We've been hit!' someone cried."

To S/2c Henry K. Willard of Washington, D.C., it had been a "pretty well muffled sound." That morning he had been relieved at his port-quarter 20-mm gun, had finished breakfast, and was en route up toward the hangar deck back to his station.

In seconds, however, he realized that the "muffled" sound belied the real seriousness of the situation as smoke began to roll around him. Instinctively, he abandoned his frenzied climb toward the hangar deck and started searching for fresh air.

To Santo "Sandy" LoFurno, another aviation ordnanceman from Rochester and friend of Joe Gruttadauria's, it was like "hitting a stone wall."

The catastrophe caught crewmen in almost as many dif-

ferent photographic stop-motions as there were those aboard.
Robert Gregg, for example, thirty-two-year-old chief bos'n's
mate also from Kansas City, was just about to remove his
overnight whiskers. With razor halfway up to his stubble, he
heard the blast and reflected almost ruefully, "Looks like I
won't shave today."

Joe Lafferty, who had been talking with the man from
Naval Personnel about wearing his helmet, was conscious of
an explosion and then an incredible thing; the man "disappeared in a flash of light."

Next, as Joe would recall:

> I felt the sting of searing flames over my face, neck, and
> arms. The concurrent explosion pushed me into a som-
> ersault and all the men in that room. . . . I found myself
> crawling along the deck yelling, "My God! I'm blind!"
>
> I could hear the flames roaring and the heat was
> unbearable. I stuck to the deck. I could see very slightly
> out of one eye. The other eye was full of blood. My
> right foot was hanging off, by my instep. My left leg was
> wide open at the calf—a large piece of shrapnel was
> sticking out. I had a large piece of shrapnel stuck in my
> forehead at the hairline.
>
> I crawled along the deck until I found a ladder.
> There were others at this ladder and every time I tried
> to climb someone pulled me back down and went up.
>
> I managed to pull myself up to the top deck. I was
> covered with blood and the skin on half my body was
> burned off.

George Cheney, who had lost in the draw for CIC watch,
was on his way to the wardroom when his own day's schedule
was shattered. He could not know at once how lucky he had
been to have lost. All but one of the forty officers and men in
CIC had been wiped out, including two staffers of Admirals
Davison and Bogan. The officer who escaped happened to be
wearing his helmet; most had suffocated.

A semidistant "bang" and a clattering of glass from broken light fixtures announced to those lingering in the wardroom that something had happened. Chaplain O'Callahan joined other officers in diving under tables, even as their allies in London pubs did during air raids.

The priest reflected with disbelief on his preoccupation a short moment ago with "fried bread" as smoke rolled through the ventilators. The words of absolution began drumming through his mind, *"ego auctoritate Ipsius vos absolvo . . ."* Mathematician even now, Father Joe calculated his chances of survival to be approximately one in twenty.

Frightened men streamed into the wardroom which otherwise was sacred officers' country, first in knots of three and five, then by the dozens. For no readily apparent reason, silence descended. One, however, who did not wait to learn what was going to happen next was Lt. Cdr. Thomas Jethro Greene of Beaumont, Texas, the engineering officer, who had just pushed back from his empty plate. As a matter of fact, Tommy had been one of those joining in the banter about the "fried bead."

Greene, a 1930 Annapolis graduate, would report:

> I proceeded to my stateroom to get my flashlight and then started through the port passageway by the ship's offices. I got as far as the turn at the navigation office and was met with a blast of intense heat. There were no lights to be seen along there.
>
> I turned back and as I turned into the athwartship passageway by the wardroom pantry I noticed a billowing cloud of smoke and flame coming from the ladder space just forward of the officers' washroom to port of the wardroom. As I ran by the pantry, GQ was sounded.
>
> I descended to the third deck via the scuttle at the foot of the ladder at Frame 74. By the time I got to the warrant officers' mess, nearly everyone had left except for a few people closing WT [watertight] doors. By

this time smoke was bad in the mess halls. There were
no lights aft of the warrant officers' mess. I spent time
trying to find a way to get in communication with the
engine room but was unsuccessful.

Kermit Clingerman, the young seaman first class from
Berea, Ohio, was caught in his own messing compartment,
testament to the many eating areas, formal and impromptu,
spotted throughout the long ship.

"Benches upset," he would recall, "trays clattered and
everybody made a rush for the nearest exit. I immediately
became aware of the fact that I was without a life jacket and
despaired at the thought. Any other time I would have been
loaded down with gear."

His battle station was on the hangar deck. Other watches
he had stood were located in fire control plot, the Mark 51
director, or on the bridge. Somehow, he never entertained
the possibility of being able to reach any of these.

As he rationalized:

I realized that it would be senseless to run or get
hysterical, so I made my way to the nearest hatch trying
to keep as calm as I could in spite of the fact that my
heart was pounding.

About that time, the bugler woke up and blasted that
dreadful sound through the ship's PA system—general
quarters! General quarters! General quarters! As if anyone cared by that time whether he even had a battle
station or not!

I saw a fellow I knew in the next compartment. He
was lying on the deck with blood oozing from one side,
and the white, sickening look on his face photographed
itself on my mind. Someone got a stretcher, then several
others started carrying him aft toward sick bay.

After making a trip up to the second deck and decid-
ing that conditions were worse up there than on the

third, I came back to the third deck and went forward
two more compartments.

He ended up in the third deck messing compartment
where he had been originally. There he found the assistant
ship's surgeon, Dr. James L. Fuelling of Westburn, Indiana,
exhorting the men to "rest quietly, conserve the limited air,
and pray."

Dr. Fuelling, a 1937 graduate of Indiana University Medical School, had been talking with Dr. Fox when the carrier
was hit. Since sick bay was not his battle station, he left, but
never progressed any farther than the starboard compartment, now gradually filling with men.

Later he would recall:

> Being the senior officer present, I took charge and
> had all doors secured, plugged up the air ducts, and
> opened the small outside vent in the outer bulkhead.
> This 4-inch opening was our only source of fresh air.
> Surrounding us in adjacent compartments were rockets
> and bombs which had been brought up from storage
> below to be delivered to the hangar deck and the flight
> deck. Many of these were loose and rolling around.

In an after mess hall Jack Grove, the young aviation ordnanceman from Frederick who had survived the Kamikaze
attack, had been eating beans and eggs. He heard not so
much a bang as a "whooshing sound" and thought some
Tiny Tims had ignited prematurely. Others had surmised
"some boob" had dropped one.

Then, as debris began to shower in through an open
hatch, there wasn't much doubt as to what had happened.
The noise and clatter increased, so as to suggest a surface
engagement.

Some men rushed forward, others aft, although the choice of escape routes was limited by the shutting of watertight doors. Grove could not get to his battle station on the hangar deck—where as a matter of fact, he would have been except he hadn't felt like waiting in the long chow line—because of the watertight integrity.

Beside him was his friend, Chief Aviation Ordnanceman Eugene Harrison, a survivor of the *Lexington*, who observed, "The damn thing's going down!"

It seemed a reasonable enough remark.

The two men put wet handkerchiefs to their faces, since smoke was now pouring down into the compartments, and started moving forward. The murk was so thick that Grove found himself within three feet of a light bulb before he was aware of its presence. One man walked head-on into a pipe.

Since they could go no farther, the pair sat down in the blackness of a compartment to wait. As they did so, they were certain they heard over a speaker: "Prepare to abandon ship!"

And then the intercom went dead.

In the confusion within the pilot house, as Quartermaster O'Donovan would later speculate, anyone might have shouted such an order into the squawk box.

While much of the individual motion was virtually aimless in its direction, some movements turned into a case of follow the leader. This was the curious happenstance attending Sandy LoFurno's peregrinations. Caught forward, just finished with some "fresh eggs," and about to go to his gun mount, he first started for sick bay to see if his friend Joe Gruttadauria was all right. He gave that idea up as impossible.

Then he noticed a man "with two holes in his side crying 'Ma!'" Sandy knew he couldn't help him but promised he'd try to locate a corpsman. Next he headed for the officers' mess hall, discovered his passage blocked by smoke and flame, and explored another direction.

Soon he had the feeling he was being followed. He turned to find about sixteen men behind him who had been keeping up with his various twistings and turnings.

"Look, fellow," Sandy confessed to a whimpering giant of a seaman directly behind him. "I don't know where'n hell I'm going either!"

During this time, several thousand yards distant from the carrier, the *North Carolina* was informing the task group, incorrectly, "*Franklin* hit by a suicider and is burning fiercely."

The damaged warship could not receive the message since her communications system had been knocked out. Signal halyards had been burned and carried away. Searchlights were shattered or otherwise inoperative. The intercom was dead, as were the various radio circuits, the range of some— the TBS type—extended no farther than the horizon.

The big radar screen on the mainmast had half toppled and the radar dome was smashed by the foretopmast which lay, it appeared to the imaginative Jurika, "like a wounded gladiator, threatening to crash down onto the navigating bridge at any moment."

Very few aboard other than Steve Jurika, who had seen the bombs slanting down after the Judy slipped out of the low clouds, were able to come to conclusions much more accurate than the *North Carolina's*. "Suiciders," or Kamikazes, were the order rather than the exception in Japan's last-gasp desperate aerial warfare.

None yet knew that the first missile, after slamming through the airplanes forward on the flight deck, had ripped through 3-inch armor to the hangar deck, or that the second had smashed aft down two decks, exploding on the third, near the chief petty officers' quarters.

Gehres, stunned and confused, thought that the ship had been damaged on the starboard side. He ordered a turn in that direction and speed slowed to two-thirds in order to put the wind on the port bow. The captain hoped thereby to prevent a fanning of the flames, especially in the vicinity of the gassed-up aircraft.

The opposite was the result as smoke wreathed the entire carrier.

When George Cheney emerged on the fo'c'sle he got the notion that the carrier was being shelled. The illusion was caused by aircraft bombs blown into the water, where some of them exploded.

Wrong impressions, understandably, predominated. Although the list was never excessive—perhaps fifteen degrees at the most—there were those who harbored the irrational fear that the *Franklin* would keep on "leaning" until she capsized.

Gun captains, unable to receive orders and concerned over the diminishing water pressure on the fire mains, began to jettison ammunition over the sides. Many of their crews had already been blown a distance of twenty feet into the water. In fact, the *North Carolina*, notifying Cruiser Division 16 that an estimated eighty men were in the water, recommended that a destroyer pick them up. The *Hickox* replied she was "standing by," about to do so.

Many, such as Chief Pharmacist Mate Norman E. Titus, who had been an embalmer in Indianapolis, were caught in fiery areas or felt they were cut off, so they jumped with little hesitation. Titus leaped into the sea from the fantail, where napalm bombs were exploding.

Harry Stinger, from Philadelphia, also a pharmacist mate, dove into the water through a flaming circle of gasoline, almost like some circus stunt. Luckily, he surfaced in the clear.

Another who attempted to slide down a rope from the

same area was far less fortunate. His leg caught in the line, and he hung there, dipping in and out of the water with the ship until he drowned.

S2/c Abe Barbash, from Tremont Avenue in the Bronx, was one of the others caught on the fantail. Abe, famed among his shipmates for running an almost nonstop (except when on duty) poker game in the laundry and quite advantageously, had never learned to swim, else he might have graduated from quartermaster school. He also possessed an unconquerable fear of heights.

When a young seaman with both arms broken was carried out of the hangar area onto the fantail, Abe took off his own life jacket and laced it around the injured youth, who was lowered into the sea away from the explosions on the fantail. Abe then decided, in view of his lack of swimming ability, that he'd better locate another life jacket, even though he might not be able to muster sufficient courage to jump into the sea. He returned inside the hangar deck—and directly into the explosion of a 500-pound bomb. As a buddy would recall, "Not even his dog tags were ever found."

Another seaman, William Fauburger, who was unable to swim and who did not take the time to look for a life jacket, jumped anyhow. He plummeted into the propeller wash, was tumbled about in the cold darkness of the water as though in a giant clothes washer. Finally, he surfaced, right next to a raft. He seized it and was assisted aboard by survivors already perched on it.

Fireman Rocco J. Caputo, from Union City, New Jersey, stayed on the fantail for almost an hour tossing jackets and other seemingly floatable material into the water until finally he decided he'd better take the plunge himself.

Below decks, the desperate fight for life—and open air—continued.

Warrant Electrician J. J. Wolf of Boston, at an electrical board, watched one man climb an escape hatch only to be

blown down again by a sharp blast. Two more tried with the
same result. One man, critically injured as he tumbled back,
died as Wolf held onto him: "I felt his hands slipping away
from me. . . ."

Then, Wolf made another attempt. He directed the beam
of his flashlight ahead of him and crawled upwards. Suddenly, as he, too, was losing his grip, hands reached out and
hauled him to safety.

Much farther down than Wolf's electrical board—in the
engine spaces—Ens. William B. Hayler of Muncie, Indiana,
a classmate of Jortberg's, had felt the bomb impacts

> as though a giant sledgehammer had been cut loose on
> the deck above us. This was followed by a very short
> lull, and then the sledgehammer, with a dozen more,
> started in again.
>
> The forced-air blowers were shut down immediately,
> but heavy smoke drifted in through the ventilating sys-
> tem so that a man could not see more than five feet.
> Almost all phones went dead and any news of what was
> going on was sketchy.

"Wild Bill" Hayler's personal belief was "that the ship's
luck had run out and that we were being nailed by Jap dive
bombers. Thoughts of home, graduation, leave, the last few
days in San Francisco, and wasted opportunities flashed by."

No. 2 fireroom (one of four), its uptakes or flues shattered
by explosions, went out of commission, the fires under its
boilers extinguished by the first blasts.

Only one phone line remained to link the engine spaces
with the bridge. That one, voice-powered and not especially
effective, ran to the aft steering control station and thence
amidships again to the main engine control. The latter was a
steel grating platform within sight of the turbines, boilers,
and other machinery containing an impressive assortment of

instruments, gauges, and levers—the brain of the carrier's propulsion system.

Among the many members of the "black gang" caught below was S2/c S. Aaron Gill from Hunt, Virginia, in No. 1 fireroom. About an hour before he was due to be relieved, he felt the ship "shake all over." He smelled fumes and smoke coming down the ventilating system. Then the carrier tilted and he slid along the slippery, oily floor grates.

His first act was to cut back on the superheat—up to 1,200 pounds per square inch—on his two boilers and turn down the oil supply to the fires. He had no way of knowing whether so much steam would still be needed to spin the turbines. If not, the pressure had to be relieved by other means.

With emergency lantern and an oxygen breather, Gill moved up a couple of levels to check on potential exits. When he opened a manhole hatch, he saw "flames all around" on the other side. He realized he would have to remain in his present situation.

Imprisoned as they were, the engine crew's situation was not as critical as that of others on board. Crewmen were cut off by fire and smoke from exits all over the carrier. This had become true of sick bay, containing Dr. Bill Fox, his seven pharmacist mates, and the remaining majority of his original eleven patients. Sensing a worsening situation, Dr. Fox, seconds after the initial bomb hit, had ordered, "All who can walk get out of here!"

Joe Gruttadauria and two or three of the patients were then led out of the ward by Hospital Corpsman John Epting and into another lower compartment through the ship's store. A group of about 150 had already gathered in this area.

Epting wished his erstwhile patients luck and returned to sick bay to care for those individuals who were still bedridden. Joe and the others had been removed none too soon. The hospital was already suffocating with heat and smoke from the hangar deck just above. The steel bulkheads were no better than sides of ovens.

Nonetheless, believing the chances of those remaining in sick bay to be as good as anywhere else, the surgeon, aided by Corpsman Epting, started placing wet towels over the faces of the patients. Valves on the oxygen flasks were turned open to supply "tents" as an aid for breathing.

Dr. Fox, however, no longer had a choice. The intensity of the fires had accelerated so much that the exit was now blocked. A chief shipfitter, Benjamin M. Durrance, a patient who had elected to remain, donned a breather, found an acetylene torch in a nearby locker, and went to work in an effort to burn through a new escape passage.

Two small overboard discharge holes had been left open —but they should not have been. Dr. Fox as well as his mates knew better. The escaping warm air kept drawing out the oxygen, with no more available for replenishment.

In the compartment on the third deck Kermit Clingerman thought that now there were upwards of 300 men who had arrived "from both directions, fore and aft." It was like a rabbit trap into which one could enter but not escape; they dared not attempt to venture into a yet more uncertain outside. With fire doors closed, there weren't too many available exits. "Every time the hatch opened," Clingerman continued, "smoke would roll in and everyone would yell, 'Close the hatch!' or 'Open the hatch!' I found a foul-weather jacket and knelt to pray."

He and his shipmates were led in prayers by Dr. Fuelling himself, as he paused in treating a wounded man, hoping to stave off panic: "Our Father who art in Heaven . . ."

Clingerman felt "nauseated" and wondered if his prayers were not "futile." Fear "shook" his soul and seemed to prevent him from drawing in what little oxygen remained in the packed place. Visions of suffocation and fire filled his mind. He later wrote:

> Then Bill Farrell, a yeoman from the exec's office, stumbled in the forward hatch. His face was black with smoke and he gasped for air and water. One of his shoes was missing and the skin was peeled off the palm of his left hand. He came over and sat down beside me asking if I could give him some water.
>
> I had no water to give him, but I tried to comfort him as best I could and told him to pray. I promised God that if He would save my life, I would be what He wanted me to be. I felt then that, if I should live, someday I would have to die, and I realized that the hour when I die will be the most important moment in my life; for it matters tremendously whether or not all is well with your soul when you are at the point of death.

A signalman, R. A. Wood, Jr., of Fresno, California, saw the faces of two men through the small glass in a hatch. They appeared to be suffocating. He knew what happened every time a door was opened, but he undogged this one anyhow and let the pair in.

The two entered, wreathed in new clouds of smoke. Coughing and choking, they collapsed on the deck.

In the instant the hatch was open, two men went out, and soon returned with buckets of dirty water. It was used to dampen handkerchiefs through which the group breathed, somewhat filtering the smoke and fumes.

Charles Loftus of Pittsburgh experienced an unusual deliverance. A machinist's mate third class, Loftus was among the relatively few asleep in their bunks when the carrier was hit. Blown out of it and onto the deck, he stumbled to his feet, grabbed his helmet and gas mask, then ran for his battle station which was the repair shop.

He soon discovered he couldn't get there. Pausing in a

compartment with others, he watched the paint on the bulk-heads "blistering" from the heat in adjacent areas. Then, as elsewhere, "the smoke became suffocating."

In a few more moments the impossible happened. A rocket detonating in the compartment ahead ruptured a large water main, doused the fires, and opened up a passage-way through which Loftus and the others made their exit.

Joe Taylor, meanwhile, was still attempting to find the bridge. He started through the smoke of the flight deck once more:

> . . . I bumped into Lieutenant J. S. Walker [of St. Louis] and we held onto each other while we made our way back to the island through the almost impenetrable pall of smoke, partially crawling so I could follow the deck seams and not lose my bearings.

Somewhere along his new course the executive officer lost his companion but encountered "several officers and men endeavoring to get a fire hose started. I helped them get it going and then managed to work my way to the starboard sponsons again and found a chain ladder leading to the bridge."

He then "scrambled up to the bridge," and "to my intense relief found the captain uninjured. He certainly hadn't lost his sense of humor because the first thing he told me was, 'Joe, I'll have to say the same thing the admiral told me when you were last bombed. Your face is dirty as hell!' "

Taylor replied, "This time it is a bit worse, though, cap-tain."

"It is, indeed," Gehres rejoined soberly.

This pleasantry had the effect of somewhat relieving the exec's tension. Not much was amusing. Although uninjured, Gehres was practically overcome by smoke and "almost to his knees," it appeared to Taylor. He coughed violently and held a small rag to his face.

A member of Admiral Davison's staff stood beside Gehres, which caused the exec to speculate that the two were discussing the possibility of abandoning ship.

Actually, Davison's chief of staff, Captain Russell, had been sent up from the flag bridge, itself almost untenable, via an emergency chain and metal rung ladder on the outside of the superstructure, with "the compliments of the admiral." He bore the crucial suggestion that Gehres turn the carrier into the wind.

Russell could not help but be aware of the changed relationship since he had been a squadron commander under Gehres in the Aleutians.

Steve Jurika, the navigator, also thought the vessel should be turned into the wind. He could see "through occasional breaks in the heavy pall of smoke enveloping us the carrier *Bataan*, apparently at full speed, also turning to starboard and crossing ahead, clear by only a few hundred yards."

He would note as well that "At this time, 0711, the ship was still making twenty-four knots and had complete steering control." However, "The entire ship was wreathed in choking smoke. Breathing was difficult, and eyes choked with tears from irritating smoke made vision doubly impossible."

Gehres took the joint advice of Russell and Jurika. He directed his command onto a course 355 degrees—due north —which put "relative wind on the starboard bow" and allowed the fire fighters to start working from fore to aft.

The situation aft was critical, partly caused by a ruptured 3-inch gasoline line, feeding the flames like a frenzied pyromaniac.

The source of information about conditions in the stern section was a group of five enlisted men in the after steering station, shielded from the fires but nonetheless trapped. Not only might the steering of the ship fall to their emergency station, but also they were serving the vital function of sole communication relay to the engine room—in fact, they were the only more or less intact communication system aboard.

With Seaman Holbrook "Brookie" Davis in charge, they hung on, even though bulkheads about them were "warming up."

Meanwhile, the lull of which those in the wardroom had been conscious had not lasted long. Explosions of bombs, rockets, and gasoline tanks commenced and continued, it seemed to Gehres, "like strings of firecrackers." They were, in Jurika's description, "soul-shaking."

As he later described it:

> The ship shuddered, rocked under the impacts, and would emerge from a period of vibration only to be rocked by another heavy blast. Fifty-caliber ammunition in the planes on deck set up a staccato chattering and the air was well punctuated with streaks of tracer. Twenty- and forty-millimeter ammunition next joined in the cacophony of sound, as the gallery mounts caught fire.

Then, Tiny Tims from the Corsairs parked aft on the flight deck took off with "an eerie whooshing sound." Jurika saw two pass by the bridge off to starboard, strike the sea, and ricochet for several hundred yards. Others launched themselves horizontally the length of the flight deck.

The navigator raced into the pilot house for shelter. He continued: "Just as I was about to emerge from the pilot house a forty-mm ready-service magazine aft on the port side erupted."

Others guessed that a big 5-inch magazine had blown.

The volcanic force lifted the *Franklin* and spun her sharply to starboard. A burst of flame nearly 400 feet high leaped from the deck edge. The flight deck was ruptured in a dozen places, like the jagged edges of monster tin cans. Those planes which were not already shattered now burst into flames. The carrier's plight was especially obvious to those aboard other ships in the group.

"When I saw those explosions," observed a seaman on the destroyer *Marshall*, "I would not have given a plugged nickel for her chances."

Once more, officers and men not directly in the path of the blast lay down on the decks to find what little air remained unpolluted by smoke.

Arthur Joseph Clarke of Richmond, Virginia, a chief photographer assigned to this voyage to film the Tiny Tims for evaluation, had much more subject matter screaming past his lenses than he could possibly record. He had mounted a big Mitchell camera on a tripod. A 16-mm camera was slung around his neck.

The order was passed to jettison everything on deck. When the photographer demonstrated his reluctance, a club-swinging master-at-arms growled, "That means you, Mac!"

And over the side went instrument and tripod, as Clarke mourned, "All five thousand dollars in the drink." However, he resumed with hand-held camera and his remaining 400 feet of 16-mm film. Every time he started to shoot, he recalled, "a bomb would go off and scare hell out of me."

Clarke found himself interrupting the filming to restrain crewmen from jumping wildly into the sea. One seaman climbed a derrick, poised himself, then dove, as Clarke would observe, "quite gracefully" into the churning waters. Since the ship was still moving at a good speed there was great danger from the propellers and backwash.

Another of the same skill, Photographer Mate 2c Charles Herbstreith from Nutley, New Jersey, was asleep in a chair in the photo lab when he was abruptly blown across the compartment. Next to him, Chief Photographer Luke Durante was instantly killed.

As Herbstreith struggled out of the shattered lab, another explosion tore off all of his clothes, leaving him with only one shoe. Otherwise, although knocked out for a time, he wasn't in especially bad shape.

One of those on the Fly 1 area of the island, a flight controlling station, was an officer whose life had proven exceptionally charmed. Survivor of the torpedoing of the *Intrepid* and, later, the bombing of the *Enterprise*, Lt. Cdr. MacGregor Kilpatrick, skipper of Fighting Squadron 5, had accidentally ridden down on one of the supply hoist elevators on the side of the flight deck seconds before the bomb hit.

Many who missed him were sure he would never be seen again.

New York–born Mac, stocky and outgoing, had graduated five years previously from the U.S. Naval Academy, where he had been All-American soccer captain. When he walked up through the island after his disappearance, to some of the men on board it seemed like a resurrection.

Now, with the smoke beginning to clear again, Kilpatrick became convinced that the "*Franklin* was on her way under." He figured, "If I was going swimming I might as well have some cash." So he started below for his quarters by the roundabout way of the foredeck, which happened to be only relatively less fireswept than the aft.

"Big Ben" puts to sea the first time, February 21, 1944. (U.S. Naval Institute Photographic Collection)

USS *Franklin* (CV-13),
January 31, 1945 (National
Archives 19-N-77562)

USS *Franklin* swings into
formation while USS
Independence does listing,
south of Bonin Island in the
Pacific. (National Archives
80-G-280293)

A Corsiar bomber taxies in. (National Archives 80-G-431196)

Captain Leslie Gehres
(National Archives
80-G-431199)

Capt. Jim Russell, Admiral Davison's
chief of staff, arrived from the flag
bridge bearing "the compliments of
the admiral"—and the urgent
suggestion that Captain Gehres turn
the carrier into the wind, to clear the
decks of smoke. (U.S. Navy Photo)

Chief Photographer Luke Durante
poses for one of himself.

Dr. George W. Fox (center) seems
to have accidentally exchanged
jackets with Chief Signalman Harry
Reese (left).

These photographs were made at a party in Bremerton prior to the *Franklin's*
return to the Pacific. The carrier was being repaired for earlier damage. Neither
Durante nor Dr. Fox survived.

An accident prior to the engagement—the pilot did not survive.
(National Archives 80-G-431158)

A twin gun mount burns furiously
after the Japanese bomber attack.
(U.S. Naval Institute Photographic
Collection)

Planes waiting to take off from the
Franklin's flight deck were consumed
by the flames. (U.S. Naval Institute
Photographic Collection)

The flight deck burns furiously while *Franklin* crewman work frenziedly with fire hoses. (National Archives 80-G-273891)

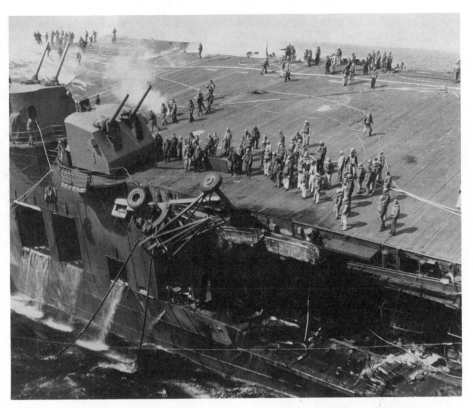

All manner of debris had to be jettisoned including the "Beast"—the shattered crane which had been used to pick up wrecked aircraft. (National Archives 80-G-273890)

The *Franklin* ablaze and dead in the water. (National Archives 80-G-273894)

The *Franklin* burns
furiously, from the area
of her island all the
great length to her
fantail. From some
apertures fire is cascad-
ing out, from others
water. The photograph
illustrates why it was
so difficult to abandon
ship even for those
who desired to do so.
(National Archives)

Crewman of the cruiser *Santa Fe* watch as they haul close to the *Franklin*, her forward flight deck crowded. Note some crewmen are wearing blankets against the cold. (National Archives 80-G-273880)

The cruiser *Sante Fe*, valiantly close, fights the fires on the *Franklin*. (National Archives 80-G-273888)

The hangar deck of the *Franklin*
—a charnel house (National
Archives 80-G-273901)

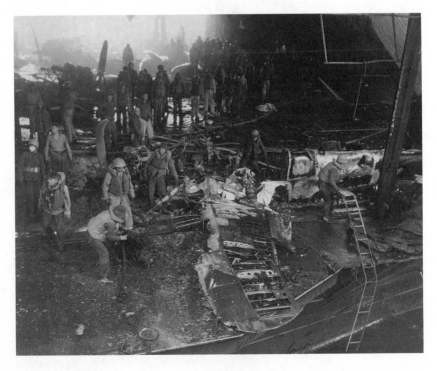

A wounded sailor is removed from the stricken carrier (U.S. Naval Institute Photographic Collection)

Lt. Cdr. Joseph O'Callahan (CHC), USNR, administers the last rites to an injured crewman aboard the *Franklin*, March 19, 1945. (U.S. Naval Institute Photographic Collection)

One of the hundreds of wounded —Seaman Joe Pennington in the *Santa Fe*'s sickbay. (National Archives 80-G-49237)

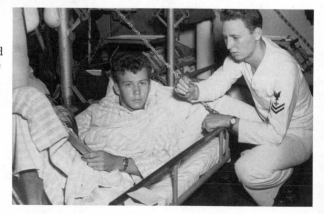

Budd Faught, a Marine pilot, the only survivor from a ready room group aboard, who had a remarkable salvation despite hours in the water—but at the cost of a leg. (Carroll Faught Photo)

The *Franklin* off U.S. shores during the long voyage home. Note the gaping holes where plane elevators should be. (National Archives 80-G-274014)

Journey's End—New York City. There wasn't much left of *Franklin*'s flight deck. (National Archives 80-G-K-4760)

Medal of Honor Winner Don Gary, extreme left, taken in 1973. (Author's Collection)

4

A "ROMAN HOLIDAY" DISPLAY

Minutes after the bombs had struck, the "soul-shaking" explosions had accounted for some 90 percent of the casualties the *Franklin* would sustain. The 500-pounder that had penetrated to the hangar deck had, like a fast fuse, triggered gasoline and ammunition. It detonated in a towering fireball to roar the cavernous length of the hangar.

Instantly killed were hundreds of men at and in their planes and others waiting in the same place in snaking breakfast lines, where Jack Grove hadn't wanted to put up with the long delay.

In ready room No. 51, a few partitions removed from CIC on the gallery deck, where only one had survived, twelve pilots who had been awaiting the strike, dressed in their Mae West jackets with helmets and headsets in their hands, died instantly, crushed in the upsurge of deck against the overhead, or ceiling. The briefing officer, who had been standing before the blackboard pointing at targets, perished with his audience in this charnel house.

There was just one exception: Budd Faught from Wyoming, who had been standing close to a bulkhead, or wall, to study a map. He had never felt confident of navigation and always tried to memorize the mission's plot. He was thus spared the full force of the mushrooming or buckling of the floor.

Nonetheless, as he lay on the deck, he realized that both his legs were broken, and also one arm—"I could hear them crumpling when they went." All was black and smoky, until he laboriously crawled a few inches along his precarious perch, then peered down a hole which he thought was "a glimpse of hell."

It was. He was looking directly into the fiery hangar deck.

Faught kept crawling, right out of a hatch onto a catwalk on the side of the carrier, immediately below the flight deck. With the explosions continuing and semi-helpless as he was, it did not seem the best of places. But he did not know what else to do. So he stayed.

Protected by relatively thin steel bulkheads from the death which had scorched by, the occupants of the crowded wardroom realized there was now no obvious escape. But although everyone in this relatively confined space sensed incipient panic or knew the elements were present to produce it, no one broke discipline in a headlong rush.

Port, starboard, and aft hatchways all were explored. Each opened into smoke and flame. Then, unexpectedly, a commanding, assured voice sang out, "All hands stand by until we find an exit!"

It was that of an assistant engineering officer, Lt. (jg) Lindsay "Red" Morgan.

In moments, he repeated, "To get out, make your way along starboard passage forward and up to the fo'c'sle!"

The officers and men "joined the trek," according to Chaplain O'Callahan.

A lack of exits was already accounting for additional casualties. Captain Izzy Isbell, en route to command the *Yorktown*, along with fourteen members of the steward's department, suffocated because heavily dogged-down doors barred their escape. Isbell, caught in the shower when the bombs hit, and seeing flames mushroom past a porthole, had simply made the wrong choice of direction in attempting to escape. He perished with the others, all vainly attempting to move the heavy latches, coughing as their strength waned.

Many others suffocated needlessly—because they froze and did not think logically. One group of nine died at their electrical board in the engine room, overcome by noxious gases. The petty officer or officers with them knew better— knew that gases rose—and they could handily have dived down into the bilges for salvation.

One who did not forget the ABC's of survival was a thin-faced, rawboned Ohioan, Lt. (jg) Donald A. Gary, a capable veteran of thirty years at sea. An assistant engineering officer who had worked his way up through the ranks, Gary knew the compartments, hatches, ducts, and narrow passageways below decks like the rooms and hallways of his boyhood home.

His station was an evaporator and he was at it when the bombs hit. First, he ordered his seven men to the bilges, then he took off. He reasoned that it was chow time and that there could be a lot of sprung doors and a lot of men caught in darkened compartments.

Gary homed in on the third deck compartment, where Dr. Fuelling and his nearly 300 men were imprisoned, as though he were following a radio beam. He likened it to a moth being attracted by a flame—a pinprick of light in this case. He had one advantage in addition to his foot-by-foot familiarity with the carrier: he wore an oxygen breather, snatched from its bulkhead receptacle at his station, kept there for just such exigencies. He announced his presence by banging on a bulkhead with his flashlight so hard that he shattered it.

He came in through a hatch—which he at once lost track of—to hear Dr. Jim Fuelling still exhorting his men, "Don't lose your heads! Don't squander your energy! Breathe quietly." And the physician commenced another prayer.

In the dim light of emergency battle lanterns Gary recognized "a look of hope and anxiety on each man's face that I shall never forget." They also seemed "oblivious" to the sounds of exploding ammunition throughout the carrier, waiting possibly for him to pronounce the magic words which would mean salvation.

"We knew plenty was going on topside," Clingerman noted, "and it was maddening to be trapped in such a place like so many guinea pigs in a laboratory." He heard from an adjacent compartment what sounded like someone banging out the Morse code on a pipe, trying to announce his presence. But how could one get to him?

There were possibly as many as four exits to the compartment where upwards of 300 now waited. But two or three of these, by which many had entered, were now impassable because of fire or smoke. One had no choice but to remain where one was.

"It was pitch black with the sides lined with sleeping bunks," according to Robert Hanna, a seaman from Kansas City. "The smoke was so thick you gasped for breath. The bulkheads were crackling with the heat from above."

He heard not only the "commotion topside" but also "the sound of rushing water . . . for all we knew that sound was made by waves washing over us as the ship went down. We had no way of knowing it really was from fire hoses above us."

Hanna, too, prayed, but "silently—we could not use up the oxygen with spoken words."

Seaman Henry Willard, who had stopped just short of the hangar deck when the carrier was hit, had ended up in this same packed compartment. He, too, was not sure but that the ship was sinking or had been already abandoned and would be scuttled with torpedoes, as had other warships too crippled to save, including the *Lexington*. Even so, his instinct for survival prevailed and he kept reassuring himself that it was *not* sinking, and he remained relatively relaxed. This was not altogether easy, especially since there were already a few dead bodies in the compartment, possibly brought in from elsewhere.

Now a strange thing happened to Donald Gary's psyche (as he would confide years later to the author): "I got just plain scared. I froze. I waited to die with the rest of them."

And so they prayed, and they froze in their fright, and they waited. All the while the minutes ticked away.

Others caught below were doing better. O'Callahan and the wardroom group were already inching along a narrow starboard passageway, under the front section of the hangar deck. As they progressed, the passage made a sharp right jog skirting the pit of the forward elevator. They could see part of its wreckage, resting at a forty-degree angle, its heavy steel pistons "bent like hairpins."

Then another explosion interrupted their journey as "the whole ship quivered in a mighty blast." The chaplain and most of the members of his party were thrown to the deck, "and pitched one against the other." The area, he thought, became like a "corked retort full of burning gases." The men broke ranks and started to run about aimlessly.

But the group rallied to continue, Indian file, until they reached a small scuttle, or emergency opening, in a hatch leading upwards to the main deck, and from there via another ladder to the fo'c'sle.

On the bridge, Gehres, bruised but with his equilibrium recovered, watched in disbelief "airplane engines and big chunks of deck spiral through the air." Now, mindful of the five men in the aft steering station, he phoned with words similar to Gary's in the messroom: "Listen. Take it easy. We'll get you out of there. It may take a little time, but it's a promise."

Their situation left much to be desired. The escape hatch on which they had counted was now—unknown to them—flooded under ten feet of water, even as a slow drip-drip commenced.

As they sat in darkness listening to explosives, in semi-limbo from the rest of the carrier, one of the five thought out loud, "I don't think we ran into a minefield."

"No," answered Seaman Brookie Davis. "We got bombed."

It was more than obvious that Big Ben needed help—and fast. Yet it was far from simple for any ship to approach this "Roman Holiday" display—as the executive officer described the eruptions—much less haul alongside.

As Taylor would recall:

> Violent explosions were rocking the ship, and debris was showering all around. Flames a hundred feet high were shooting up past the island; the roar of exploding shells was deafening. A column of smoke rose a mile above the clouds. Perhaps up there the spirits of the men of the brave *Lexington*, who died in the Coral Sea, and the *Yorktown*, who perished at Midway, were waiting for the captain's words, bidding him speak.

Then, the Tiny Tims began to blow:

> Some screamed by to starboard . . . some to port and some straight up the flight deck. The weird aspect of this weapon whooshing by so close is one of the most awful spectacles a human has ever been privileged to see.
>
> Some went straight and some tumbled end over end. Each time one went off, the fire-fighting crews forward would instinctively hit the deck . . . their heroism was the greatest thing I have ever seen.

Others, taking off from the smoldering, twisted charnel

house of the hangar deck, tore through the sides of the
Franklin as though the bulkheads were constructed of card-
board and raced, leaving fiery trails, past other ships toward
the horizon.

Nonetheless, in spite of the obvious peril, the destroyer
Miller eased to within several hundred feet of the carrier's
stern and commenced playing streams of water on the fires.
She was joined by the destroyer *Hickox*.

At the opposite end, the carrier's blond fire marshal, Lt.
(jg) Stanley S. "Steamship" Graham, yelled to a group of
sooty-faced but otherwise able-bodied seamen and other rat-
ings emerging like flushed badgers from fortuitously placed
scuttles, "Boys, we got pressure on the lines, we got hoses.
Let's get in there and save her!"

The word spread there in "bow" country. Soon almost a
dozen hoses were being inched aft along the flight deck, the
crewmen using the streams of water to scatter the flames and
make slow progress across the smoking plates and burning
Douglas fir planking, which was used for carrier decks since
it did not splinter.

Men with axes chopped holes in this wood to permit water
to flow down into the blazing gallery deck compartments—
and allow more fire fighters to descend there and also into
the hangar deck area, or what was left of it. White-hot fires
of magnesium bombs glowed in the ashes and wreckage of
the planes that had carried them.

Cdr. Hale, the air officer ordered from his normal station
at fly control to take charge of fire fighting on the hangar
and flight decks, came across one young seaman playing a
hose on a steaming bomb. It perhaps had tumbled from the
rack of a plane awaiting takeoff.

Hale had arrived not a moment too soon. The stream of
water was spinning the arming valve, as though the missile
were tumbling to its target against the air and wind. It was
just about ready to detonate.

Seven 500-pound bombs, so hot they burned flesh at the touch, were rolling around the flight deck. A team of officers, a chief, and several enlisted men pushed and shoved them over the side.

Men below on the second and third decks, or trapped on the hangar deck aft, were making their way to safer zones. Dozens had been blown over the side; others, trapped, were forced to leap over, many without life jackets. Little groups struggled to the fantail, where they fought the fires with every means at their command, leaping into the water when their position became unbearable.

Then, at about 7:41, word came from a destroyer that a Zeke was "diving on the formation from stern."

An emergency turn was ordered for all ships.

5

THE ADMIRAL AND
HIS STAFF DEPART

The Zeke never made it. The enemy plane was shot down comfortably abeam of the *Franklin*.

Still, greater problems persisted, as Captain Gehres would record:

> The explosions of heavy ordnance progressively from forward aft, some of it dropping into the hangar deck to explode spread fire and destruction throughout the ship from the island down to the fourth deck.
>
> Eventually, all topside five-inch, forty-mm, twenty-mm, ready and aircraft ammunition lockers, and the ammunition in all gun lockers aft of the bridge exploded.

At about the same time, Admiral Davison requested Gehres to slow from sixteen to eight knots. He was preparing to move his staff to the *Miller* as soon as that destroyer could safely maneuver alongside. For the admiral's purposes, the *Franklin* was no longer an "effective unit." The operation might require as long as an hour.

The mechanical telegraph was rung up as Gehres obeyed the admiral: "All engines ahead one-third!"

In the lower regions of the carrier, at Central Damage
Control Station, those on duty were finding their task increasingly difficult. They normally kept a check, through a
maze of colored lights in a panel on the magazines, on fuel
tanks and the general stability of the ship. Areas of runaway
flooding should at once become apparent.

All the duty team could watch was a frustrating maze of
burned-out bulbs or a short-circuitry of flashing red lights. If
believed, the sum of the indicators added up to an inescapa-
ble conclusion: the ship, afire from stem to stern and all
magazines exploding like the biggest Fourth of July ever
conceived, was listing ninety degrees in both directions and,
as a matter of fact, should have sunk several minutes ago.
Actually the list never exceeded sixteen degrees.

Circuit breakers were hauled open. While this restored a
measure of sanity to the crazy-quilt panorama, the purpose
of the whole station was thereby defeated. The control
board was now dead.

The duty section was lucky at that. Perhaps as many as
two-thirds of the damage control team of 118 men had perished elsewhere on the ship, mostly in the breakfast line.

Finally concluding they were useless here, the men left
through an escape trunk to join the fire-fighting teams
which, they reasoned, must be in need of recruits.

The chaplain and the wardroom party were also coming
into the clear, via the fo'c'sle, with its assortment of anchors,
chains, cables, tackle, and winches. O'Callahan now de-
toured to his own room where he fitted himself with life belt,
helmet bearing the distinctive white cross, and a vial containing holy oils for the sacrament of extreme unction.

There seemed little doubt that the priest would need the
last when he entered the junior aviators' bunk room, just aft
of the fo'c'sle. Here were some thirty badly burned men,
moved in apparently from other areas of the *Franklin*.

Chaplain Gatlin, who was handy at first aid, had already

arrived. There were several pharmacist mates in attendance in this emergency ward but no doctor. Sulfa powder, burn jelly, and morphine happened to be in good supply.

"Jesus Christ!" one of the wounded cried out. Then, noticing the chaplain, he added, "I guess I owe you a dollar."

It was an unofficial rule among the Catholic members of the crew that if the padre caught any of them using profanity the culprit had to pay one dollar towards the church fund. O'Callahan moved over to the bunk. "That's free today, son," he said.

Against a backdrop of whooshing Tiny Tims, explosions, and rattlings as the ship rolled away from her starboard list and then back into it again, O'Callahan worked and prayed over the most seriously hurt of the patients. Then, after a quick conference with Gatlin, the Catholic priest decided that he'd better move around to ascertain who else might be in need of aid.

O'Callahan left via the outside starboard passage, hugging the bulkheads to avoid being thrown overboard by the next explosion. The noise somehow "seemed more terrible." He speculated as to whether this was only relatively so since right now he was not preoccupied with tending others.

A little distance along the way he spoke to a man whose "eyes did not focus, jaws sagging," but who showed no visible signs of hurt. He passed another and another—all victims of shock.

The smoke all about him appeared to the chaplain like the "shroud mantling a dead ship . . . the flames, snake-tongued, writhing high into the sky or lashing fore and aft, port and starboard, scourging those who thought themselves safely distant from the center of destruction. . . ."

At one exposed place the former Holy Cross mathematics professor glimpsed, through a rift in the smoke, the captain and Jurika on the bridge. He wondered why they did not leave before they might be completely trapped.

Another explosion, followed by the sound of a Tiny Tim screaming nearby, and O'Callahan was thrown to the deck. He saw "shrapnel, entire airplane engines, untold smaller chunks of steel shooting through the air—hurtling up, then pelting down."

He picked himself up, then glanced apprehensively at the island. To his surprise, he noted that the structure, Gehres, and his navigator were still there—like a contemporary Fortress McHenry during the British bombardment.

The priest ended his journey on the forward part of the flight deck where Dr. Sam Sherman, a flight surgeon from San Francisco, was working over "burned, mangled, and bleeding bodies." They were obvious terminal patients such as the physician had never seen before in his practice—at least not in one, frightful mass.

"Dr. Sam," as a matter of fact, was only now recovering his second wind after being knocked unconscious by the first blast. Standing on the flight deck, he had been hurled against the island structure.

It was cold, for the carrier continued to move ahead into the wintry winds of Japan's Home Islands. O'Callahan decided his positive contribution of the moment would be to organize blanket parties. Noticing two or three seamen standing around, bewildered, he snapped out an order to them:

> Here, lads, go down the forward catwalk, go immediately below to the gallery bunk room. Each of you get two helpers and all of you bring up blankets. If you can't find fifty blankets, bring up mattresses—and quick! Go now . . . !

As O'Callahan turned his attention to the dying, an aviator was organizing activity commensurate with the importance of the blanket brigade. Mac Kilpatrick, who had retrieved his "cash" in anticipation of "swimming," was still dry, and very busy.

Joe Taylor, who had observed that almost all of the gun platforms were flaming and their ready box ammunition blasting off with fury and regularity depending on the particular mount, asked Kilpatrick to organize a party to jettison shells from a forward 5-inch-38. Since shell and projectile came in two pieces and the latter weighed perhaps fifty pounds, the task was something less than simple.

En route, Mac paused to lend a hand to a group having difficulty loading two hot 1,000-pound bombs into a cart. Somehow, they succeeded, trundled them to the deck edge and watched the big missiles drop sizzling into the sea.

The executive officer, having hurried several other ammunition dumping parties after Kilpatrick, was ordered by Gehres to make a personal "estimate" of how things were "proceeding" below.

As Taylor later recalled it:

> Upon reaching the flight deck, I found a large group of men huddled on the port bow and at this point it was becoming difficult to get men to spell each other on the hoses.
>
> I tried to shout orders but found that I couldn't even get out anything more than a hoarse whisper. Several officers and myself grabbed hoses which were not tended and this brought some of the men out of the huddle to help us.
>
> I next made my way to the forecastle, which was becoming very crowded by surviving personnel. I went aft through the officers' country on the forecastle deck and got my first look at the hangar. All hoses available were playing on the fires in the forward part of the hangar and seemed to be making considerable progress.
>
> The hangar deck was a nightmare of death and destruction. Bodies were everywhere, in the passageways,

on the ladders where they had dropped, one hanging
from a catwalk on the overhead by one arm. The
center bay sprinklers were apparently going full blast.
Wounded were being rushed to the forecastle deck and
many were temporarily placed in staterooms in this
area.

At 7:47 the new heavy cruiser *Santa Fe* was ordered to
proceed to the *Franklin* to take charge of emergency operations as well as of fighter plane direction. Her veteran commanding officer, trim Capt. Harold C. Fitz, Annapolis, 1920,
was more than ready and able to carry out any rescue.

At the same time, Hal Fitz, who had been a three-star
athlete at the Academy, was aware of earlier and tragic assistance operations in the war, particularly the case of the
Birmingham which suffered 649 casualties while maneuvering alongside the burning *Princeton* in October 1944 at
Leyte Gulf. The cruiser's decks had been swept from stem to
stern by a massive explosion aboard the doomed carrier.

Then, shortly after 8 A.M., less than an hour after the
Franklin had been hit, the *Santa Fe* logged:

> Set condition I in all repair parties. Rigged all fire
> hoses topside and broke out mooring lines in prepara-
> tion for going alongside *Franklin* to extinguish fires and
> rescue survivors.
>
> As we approached the burning ship we again ob-
> served a trail of men in the water. Destroyers were busy
> picking them up but there were so many that the de-
> stroyers fell far behind.
>
> As we passed survivors, life jackets, life rings, rafts,
> and floater nets were thrown over to take care of the
> men until the destroyers could come up.

Aboard the carrier, Admiral Davison was ready to leave.
He came into the pilot house distributing surplus cartons of

mentholated cigarettes. As Gehres would note officially, "Commander Task Group 58.2 told me to pass the word to prepare to abandon ship."

Then, in eloquent understatement, the captain continued, "No action was taken on this, but the admiral was requested to provide surface and air support and we would save the ship."

Steve Jurika, still at the side of the captain, was himself quite certain that "Prepare to abandon ship!" never was passed. Gehres, however, used his lusty voice to order, "Stand by to transfer all wounded and evacuate all unnecessary personnel not required to fight the ship!"

John O'Donovan, quartermaster of the watch in the pilot house, became intrigued by the "final colloquy between Davison and Gehres." O'Donovan would later write (to the author):

> The admiral came into the pilot house and motioned to the captain to join him over at the chart table on the port bulkhead. Neither one noticed a certain QM 2/c with big ears standing within a foot of them, apparently absorbed in watching the inclinometer.
>
> "Captain," said the Admiral, "I think there's no hope." Gehres nodded, said nothing. "I think you should consider abandoning ship—those fires seem to be out of control," continued the admiral.
>
> Once more, Gehres nodded, said nothing. With that, they shook hands, wished each other luck and the admiral left the pilot house.

This did not reflect a subordinate's disregarding an implied order of a superior. As O'Donovan would rationalize:

> Under Navy protocol a task group or task force commander commands a group of ships but, in a certain sense, does not directly command any one ship in the

group. . . . Davison could order the *Franklin* to under-
take any task within the operational possibilities of an
aircraft carrier. But he could not order Gehres to abandon ship.

The decision to abandon or to try to save the *Franklin*
is a decision reserved to the commanding officer of the
Franklin. The Navy put the ship in his hands. He and
he alone was answerable to the Navy for whatever
might happen to her.

As a matter of fact, Davison was an old hand at leaving
this carrier. He had done so the past year after the Kamikaze
attack.

At 8:20 the *Miller* was alongside the *Franklin*.

The duty officer of the destroyer wrote in his log with
evident surprise that crewmen from the burning carrier were
still "jumping overboard."

It was true. The catastrophe that had befallen the *Franklin* was not yet, in Navy lingo, "organized." Lt. William A.
Simon, Jr., from Wilmington, North Carolina, the only one
to survive out of nearly forty in the Combat Information
Center after an explosion below had heaved the deck upward, was miracuously unharmed and watching the pan-
demonium.

"Men were screaming," he would recall, " 'Let's go over
the side!' Through the darkness of smoke I saw about twenty-
five jump. Smoke was so thick it was more like night than
day."

One of their number was Budd Faught, who had escaped
from the doomed ready room No. 5. He had sat on the portside catwalk as the explosions seemed to "bounce" him "up
and down." He had left his life jacket in the room. All he had
was his "G" or gravity suit, which was waterproof and could
be blown up like a Mae West preserver.

Budd, who had inhaled too much smoke, had no wind to

inflate the suit. He prevailed on another officer, Capt. Robert M. Jones, his squadron leader, who had appeared beside him on the catwalk, to blow through the tube into the zipped-up suit. While Jones was burned about the face and arms and there was a strange, bloodless bruise on his forehead, he had more wind than Faught and appeared stronger.

The fires, however, came closer and the nearby outhanging port plane elevator became rocked by explosions. Finally, all manner of debris, including its outer, flexible steel covering, began blowing out seaward.

Faught decided it was past time to leave, his resolve strengthened by the fact that he was a good swimmer. With two broken legs and one fractured arm, it was not easy to move. He took hold of a part of the framework and hung on with one hand as his legs dangled.

Beneath was a burning ship's boat. He couldn't fall onto that, so he started swinging in and out like a trapeze artist. Finally, he let go.

The injured pilot went down some fifty feet—"I thought I would never hit"—plunged under, then bobbed up again. He saw a massive eruption where he had been. His buddy, Captain Jones, vanished in a puff of flame.

The water was cold. Faught used his good arm to keep pushing himself away from the side of the carrier, which he swore was hot to the touch. He had to avoid the suction and the propellers of the still swiftly moving ship.

Now came the cumbersome operation of transferring Davison, Bogan, and the flag staffs by breeches buoy over to the *Miller*. Fortunately, the seas were not too rough.

O'Callahan looked up from his exposed position forward and mused to himself that if the transfer were "awkward," so was the spectacle of two admirals leaving their ship—moreover, one which was still afloat and just might conceivably remain in that fortuitous state.

The priest rationalized, however, that Davison's duty was to direct the operation from a more secure base. Gehres' obligations were quite another matter.

In fifteen minutes Admiral Davison was aboard the *Miller*. Through radio to the task force he repeated his summary: "Am afraid we will have to abandon her. Please render all possible assistance." He then ordered the heavy cruiser *Pittsburgh*, newer and of nearly 4,000 more tons displacement than the *Santa Fe*, to maneuver in toward the *Franklin*.

Capt. John Gingrich from Dodge City, Kansas, a classmate of Hal Fitz, radioed back that he was on his way. Gingrich, known to his intimates as "Ginrickey," was not quite sure what the admiral had in mind. The *Santa Fe* seemed to be handling the situation admirably. But he altered course and plowed in anyway.

The commanding officer ordered fo'c'sles made ready for survivors and a quick inventory of medical stores. The way the *Franklin* was putting up smoke and exploding, Gingrich didn't think he could do much to save her.

And on the *Miller* Davison at last had a moment for reflection. As he would confide to his chief of staff, "I got the feeling the Japs were mad at me."

Two times they had forced him over the side in less than six months. . . .

6

"AS THOUGH SHAKEN BY AN ANGRY CAT"

About 9 A.M. the *Miller*, with the admiral's pennant waving from her forepeak, hauled away. As she passed the *Franklin's* stern, the destroyer slowed to pluck off two men who had been hanging with failing strength to ropes.

It appeared increasingly that Davison's pessimistic assessment was beyond any possibility of refutation. Explosions continued, as Taylor noted, to "rock the ship, and debris was showering all around." With each explosion there was an exceptionally violent blast and smoke rolled over the island, and those on the bridge would duck into the pilot house for the scant cover offered.

In addition to the spasmodic detonations of ammunition and rockets, tanks of aviation gasoline in the sides of the carrier were also erupting and flowing in lavalike streams into the water. This happened as the ship settled, forcing more water into the gasoline reservoirs and propelling the aviation fuel itself to the top, where there was fire aplenty to ignite the highly flammable liquid.

At 9:11 the *Franklin*, still without communication circuits, blinkered to the nearing *Santa Fe*, "We have lost steering control. Can you send fire hoses?" There was a pause, and the carrier added, "Can you send for sea tugs?"

Jack Grove and Chief Harrison, who had survived the *Lexington's* sinking, finally decided to move on from their compartment, impelled in part by someone wearing a rescue breather who came along and advised them to "go as far forward, starboard side as you can and hit the warrant officers' mess!"

They started. En route, Grove stumbled over what he thought was a body. When he gained the warrant officers' mess, he was still bothered about that "body."

"Gene," he told the chief, "he may be alive. I am not going to let him die there. Look for me in a few minutes if I don't return."

Grove found the "body" in the passageway and dragged him all the way into the mess. He was a young yeoman and quite alive, though partly overcome by smoke. Grove found an orange and offered it to him.

At that point a flight surgeon, Dr. F. Kirk Smith, appeared and said no, the orange was too acid. The surgeon, as Dr. Fuelling had elsewhere, urged all the men to "conserve" their energy and lie down if they wished.

Among others who arrived for Surgeon Smith's attention was Joe Lafferty, now badly in shock, burned and suffering from loss of blood:

> I lay on the deck while Dr. Smith treated me and bandaged my burns. He was called away, as the wounded were coming in fast. The explosions were continuing and I felt the urge to dig a foxhole in the steel deck. I lost track of time but someone said we were going to abandon ship. I tried to get up. I was completely covered with blood and the doctor hadn't noticed my legs.

Joe called Dr. Smith back who then administered further treatment to his left leg and right foot. He refused morphine as he had the irrational idea that he would pass out and be left if they abandoned ship: "I managed to get up and crawled to the forecastle where the wounded were being placed, awaiting transfer. When I got in the open, the fresh air caused me to collapse."

Meanwhile, Don Gary and Dr. Fuelling had remained for long minutes in their compartment until, finally, Gary "unfroze." Possibly it was because more and more of the assembled men were verging on panic; a few were actually screaming. The engineering officer was not at all sure how he could cope with *that*.

Gary found himself snapping out, aloud, "Damn it! We're not dead yet!"

As Dr. Fuelling recounted it (to the author), here is what happened next:

When the explosions quieted, we opened a door and found there was dense smoke about us. The air in the compartment was running low and the humidity was high. Lieutenant Gary thought he had about ten minutes of oxygen left in his apparatus and suggested he leave our compartment and find a safe way out.

He remembered the uptakes from the engine room and he proceeded forward on the third deck to a hatch going down to the fourth deck where there was an access hatch to one of the uptakes from the engine room. No air was moving in this uptake but there was not much smoke.

He crawled upward on his hands and knees to the end of the uptake (which had steel ladder rungs) where there was an opening to the outside of the island structure. He then proceeded to get a few breaths of fresh air and located a fresh oxygen canister and returned down the uptake to the fourth deck, back up to the third deck and back to our compartment. He suggested taking ten men out if they held their breath as long as possible and moved swiftly following him.

Forming a chain by holding each other's hands and breathing through a cloth such as a shirttail or handkerchief wet with coffee or urine, they left.

Gary did not want to lose more than the ten if a bomb exploded, or if he made a wrong turning to their common doom. And so he went, the first man in the chain hanging onto him, back down the same route, in smoky blackness, sometimes aided by the steel rungs, sometimes not.

Dr. Fuelling continued:

During the time Lieutenant Gary was gone I did my best to keep the men under control and to avoid panic. I did suggest they say a prayer and remain calm for we couldn't be sure when or if we would get out alive. We all hoped the ten men had reached safety but had no way of knowing whether they were able to get through.

Gary and the ten did get through, traveling the 600 up-and-down, twisting feet to one of the 40-mm gun sponsons, six decks above. All of the men were as scared as Gary claimed he had been originally. Each clutched with a death grip the hand of the next, and the chain was never broken.

Outside at last, the men collapsed, gasping for the relatively fresh air and thankful to be upon the slanting, debris-filled deck, cluttered now with hose lines.

Gary's work was not finished. He returned and led 50 more men out. The third time he prepared to guide all others to safety: the more than 200 remaining.

The escape of Kermit Clingerman was somewhat more curious. If he indeed started in one of Gary's chains he subsequently lost it and his memory persisted that "a Marine" had taken the lead position.

"Holding a handkerchief in front of my mouth with one

hand," he would recall, "and holding onto the next man's belt with the other, I went stumbling into the next compartment, which was dark and filled with smoke. I fell over an ammunition hoist, letting go of the person ahead of me."

At that point his "heart sank" and he found himself struggling loose from the grip of the person behind:

> The next thing I remember I was in one of the forward mess halls standing in warm water. There was a light ahead of me and I lost no time in getting to it. I was then in the forward mess hall where I joined several other fellows and together we made our way through officers' country and up three decks to the fo'c'sle. I was overwhelmed with joy to be alive and I thanked God from the bottom of my heart for delivering me.

He hunted for a life jacket, which was "reg" enough, even though going overboard presented its own hazardous route to salvation. He obtained one, also some flashproof clothing stored in an emergency deck locker for just such eventualities:

> In the excitement I had left my foul-weather jacket back in the compartment where I had been trapped. I walked out onto the bow of the ship and the first person I met was the Protestant chaplain. He was passing out swigs of wine to those who needed moral courage.

This somewhat surprised the teetotaler Clingerman since he associated alcohol with the convivial Father O'Callahan, not Chaplain Gatlin: "I surely was glad to see him, but I didn't appreciate his offer of a little wine."

Below, the situation had progressed from bad to worse with dramatic and frightening acceleration. One fireroom after another was going out of commission as smoke and heat made working in them intolerable. The first explosion had knocked out the furnace flames in No. 2 fireroom.

Continuing as relayer of messages from the black gang, Holbrook Davis phoned the bridge from after steering that the below-deck ventilators were out and the engine crews— machinists, electricians, water tenders, and firemen—were collapsing from smoke inhalation. They sought permission to "secure"—to close down what was not shut already—and leave.

There were not nearly enough gas masks or breathers. But the crewmen couldn't have endured the heat even if there had been sufficient oxygen face masks.

The explosions were ripping gashes in steam lines. At least one thermometer cracked at the mark of "200°."

Gehres advised Davis to tell the engineers to leave the throttles set at eight knots and to make their way topsides as best they could, without "securing station." That is, the engines should run until they stopped—which should be in about forty minutes.

Some of the firerooms received the laboriously relayed order from the weakening voice phone circuitry. Others missed it entirely. But it did not matter. The men could not endure the heat any longer. They were already groping away from their boilers, switch panels, turbines, and the big steel control wheels which regulated the amount of high-pressure steam roaring over the turbine blades.

Most of the crewmen found the customary ladder exits still passable. They arrived gasping for breath in bow areas of the ship. One group in the forward engine room called for "someone with a breather" to come to their aid, then added the plaintive signoff: "Trapped!"

The men were helped to safety within a few minutes. In an aft fireroom, however, not so affected with smoke, several hardy water tenders stuck to their posts.

Roy Treadaway of San Angelo, Texas, a nineteen-year-old fireman working for "the oil kings" of "B" division in the after auxiliary machine room, had been at his No. 5 fuel oil booster and transfer pump when the carrier was hit. He had helped to correct momentarily the starboard list by requesting and receiving permission to shift oil from the starboard to port side.

When the electricity went off and an auxiliary generator was started, an obstructed exhaust stack began to shunt carbon monoxide fumes into the compartment. Roy "prayed," even though he did not consider himself a religious man, and "cussed," but "never gave a thought to giving up!"

He later reported:

> We hastily evacuated the area without notifying anyone. We tried to make our way straight upward, but a burning 1,000-pounder bomb on the second deck made us turn back. We retreated to the mess hall on the third deck, then farther aft to the aviation engine ready shop. An engine was lying on the armored hatch that we pried open with a 2-inch bunk support. The hangar deck was greasy and littered.

Tommy Greene, who had quickly left the wardroom, had been compelled to set up an impromptu office in the warrant officers' mess. At that time, he held the opinion that he could not come any closer to his regular chief engineer's office. As it turned out, he spent most of his time helping an officer and a chief electrician who had been overcome with smoke.

A member of the medical department arrived to continue first aid. Greene then directed his attention to smoldering fires in a mess hall forward and in the adjacent ship's store. When he found that the sprinkler system, now a trickle, was "more a hindrance than a help" to those fighting the fires, he turned it off.

Aaron Gill made his escape out of No. 1 fireroom through the chiefs' quarters. Now that he had found an exit, it was surprisingly easy to make his way to safety, which happened to be the bow. The only sight out of the ordinary he encountered en route was a dead man lying quite alone on a table.

As Bill Hayler emerged from the engine spaces, he discovered "lights were out in some compartments and my flashlight beam was largely absorbed in the smoke."

After reaching the hangar area, he continued:

> I was not sure whether I was entering Dante's Inferno or crossing the River Styx. Steam rose from the hangar deck where it was being struck by water cascading down from the fire-fighting topside. More vapor rose from the little streams which carried the water across the littered deck and over the low starboard side.

He found, as Joe Taylor had before him, that the whole area was burned out, blackened, with large chunks missing from the top and sides, or bulkheads.

Hayler added:

> The forward elevator had been blown out of its well and settled back to form a ramp between the hangar and flight decks. Airplane engines were still burning fiercely and in many cases were all that remained of what once had been a complete machine capable of flight and bearing men aloft. Strewn all around was the evidence that there had been no escape for many of those who were trapped in the inferno.
>
> Worse than the hangar deck was the gallery deck between them, with its maze of narrow passageways, ready rooms, workshops, clipping rooms, and armories. After the two bomb hits, this area was like the oven of a gigantic stove.

To others, Mac Kilpatrick for one, the remnants inside this "stove" resembled "oatmeal," or "irregular cinders."

The hangar deck seized the men's imaginations and locked them momentarily in awe. O'Callahan saw it as "one solid mass of fire," with scattered airplane engines simply "coals of special brilliance." Here no one could have survived.

Then, moving to the flight deck again he watched flames "tall as towers."

About fifteen minutes after the *Miller* had drawn away, the *Santa Fe* began closing the starboard side of the *Franklin*.

"Do you know what speed you are making?" Captain Fitz inquired by blinker gun.

"Eight knots," came the reply.

He then wished to know if the magazines were flooded.

"We believe the magazines are flooded," the *Franklin* answered. "Am not sure."

This uncertainty was justified. The water valves had been turned full on. Unknown to the chief gunners mates, however, the pipes were split. Not a drop of water ever reached the hundreds of tons of explosives inside—at least those stored in the after magazines.

The *Franklin*, the *Santa Fe* logged, "had about eleven degree list to starboard, was burning fiercely aft, and a flaming gasoline fire was pouring out of the hangar deck on the starboard quarter. There were explosions from time to time."

Fifty feet abeam of the *Franklin*, the 10,000-ton cruiser adjusted her speed to maintain station with the larger vessel. One hose, then another, and still another began pouring water across the gap onto the fires. The next maneuver was to throw lines to portions of the carrier's decks less affected by the flames.

"Provision whips"—heavy lines running through pulleys at either end—were beginning to transfer the seriously wounded over the expanse of water to the *Santa Fe*.

Before the cruiser could make much headway with its several operations, however, there came, at 9:52, "an immense explosion aft on the *Franklin*," according to the watch officer aboard the *Santa Fe*. "Large sections of her hangar deck were blown up and debris was thrown all over this ship. Two fire hoses aft were cut but luckily no men were injured."

"The ship felt," as Jurika would describe it, "as though it were a rat being shaken by an angry cat."

7

"ABANDON? HELL, WE'RE STILL AFLOAT!"

Fitz ordered the cruiser to back away, which she did. All lines were severed.

O'Callahan was at a loss to understand "how we survived it." It had everyone, by a familiar service expression, "crawling into his helmet," as a hail of debris peppered the stricken ship.

Jurika, convinced it was "the most terrific blast of the morning," pinpointed its source as one of the 5-inch ready-service magazines beside a twin mount. Mac Kilpatrick and his volunteers were endeavoring, elsewhere, to jettison this same-caliber shell.

Jurika continued:

> Whole aircraft engines with propellers attached, debris of all descriptions including pieces of bodies, were flung back into the air and descended on the general area like hail on a roof.
>
> One engine and prop struck the navigation bridge a glancing blow about three feet from my head and for a couple of moments I will admit to ducking under the overhang of the masthead light.

One man, Machinist Mate 1c Louis A. Vallina of East St. Louis, Illinois, was blown off the fantail. He landed so far away from the carrier that he "didn't have to worry about getting sucked under."

Vallina held onto an empty shell container until a destroyer loomed toward him. Stunned and confused, he figured he might have been drifting toward Japan in the few minutes he was in the water, and thought the ship was unfriendly. He actually attempted to hide under his small float when the task force destroyer swept alongside to pick him up.

Roy Treadaway, too, had ended up in the sea after making good his escape from the aft auxiliary machine room. He slid down a burning 40-mm gun mount and the "next thing" he remembered was swimming and the *Santa Fe's* seamen fishing for him.

They were unsuccessful because of the suction from the propellers. The cruiser abandoned the effort and tossed life jackets to him and a companion. Soon, two other swimmers joined Treadaway as they seemed to be carried ever farther away from the *Franklin* and her escorts.

The temporary departure of the *Santa Fe* was heartbreaking to the seriously wounded awaiting transfer. There seemed to be no adequate space now on the carrier for their care.

One young sailor presented an especially pitiful sight. He lay on a stretcher, a makeshift tourniquet and bandage over the stump of a leg bathed in red. Yet he was conscious. Could he be transferred to another ship in time? And what if the *Franklin* had to be hurriedly abandoned?

As a shipmate would observe, it was "embarrassing" to have to look the casualty in the eyes and yet be unable to assist him except by trying to force out a lying reassurance.

Another disappointed casualty was Joe Lafferty, who had

lain on the flight deck while "some young kid held onto my shirt to keep me from sliding overboard." At one time, Father O'Callahan attempted to administer last rites but Lafferty refused since "I was prepared and also determined not to give up."

As the storm of shell and steel plate fragments and fireballs from the carrier's eruption somewhat abated, O'Callahan and his little group forward on the flight deck returned to their hoses. It had become one of the many fire-fighting parties that had swung into action. Noticing two men who were so still that the chaplain was certain they were dead, he commenced the last rites. He wasn't half-finished, however, when one of them stirred, coughed, and the second opened his eyes and blinked. They had been stunned, but not too seriously hurt.

If the explosion was devastating to those aboard the reeling carrier, it looked just about the same to other ships of the task force. Admiral Mitscher ordered his signalman on the *Bunker Hill* to transmit a routine permission to abandon ship, convinced that the *Franklin* was anxiously anticipating this very confirmation.

Gehres was considerably less than appreciative. He ordered his own "flags," or signalman, to reply, "Abandon? Hell, we're still afloat!"

To the rating, it hardly sounded like an official message, but orders were orders. He flashed it over to the flagship just as the captain had muttered it to him. It would take its place alongside other memorable utterances in the history of naval warfare.

Brave words to the contrary, the *Franklin* was scarcely the "effective unit" needed by Admiral Davison for his flag. At 10 o'clock the last pounds of steam pressure had fizzled to a low whine in the turbine pipes.

A few minutes later Fitz, on the *Santa Fe*, informed the

Bunker Hill, "*Franklin* now dead in water. Fires causing explosions. Have got a few men off. Fires still blazing badly . . . whether *Franklin* can be saved or not is still doubtful."

The "few men" were not nearly enough to satisfy Fitz. He would have to batter his way back through the wreckage alongside the carrier and continue the transfer. He made mental calculations, characteristically deliberate. Then, seizing his opportunity, he drove in at twenty-five knots from a wide angle, like an immense floating ram.

"She's coming fast!" someone on the carrier shouted.

She hit, bow first, knocking aside the toppled radio mast of the *Franklin,* cables, ropes, bent stanchions, all manner of debris—and held.

As the carrier shuddered under the blow, Gehres thought of the feat as "the most daring piece of seamanship I ever saw." And Jurika likened the approach to that of "a well-handled gig making a liberty float at Long Beach."

Banging side by side, the two ships were literally within speaking distance. One officer on the *Santa Fe* was quick to take advantage of the proximity. Ens. Robert S. Hayes recalled that a classmate, Jortberg, was aboard the *Franklin:*

"Dick!" he called out and was rewarded by the sight of his friend, leaning from the crazily tilting island.

"What do you hear from your wife?" Hayes asked Jortberg. He referred to the former Betty Jean Redfern. The three had been good friends at Annapolis.

Conversation, however, was drowned out by the overriding noise and continuing explosions. Boards and aluminum ladders were stretched from the *Franklin* to the *Santa Fe,* enabling the wounded to be carried down in an increasing flow. Some of them were in large mail pouches. Dr. Sam Sherman, with the air group, protested, "I'm a doctor. I can't leave the ship. You need me."

He won, and stayed. MacGregor Kilpatrick, the pilot, argued and lost.

"You are an aviator, not a fire fighter!" Gehres barked. "Take your pilots and get moving!"

Mac got moving, with the cash in his pocket he had procured from below—anticipating a swim that had proven unnecessary.

Among the more than 800 who trouped aboard the *Santa Fe* was Jack Grove. After he had caught his breath, he had rather easily left the warrant officers' mess through a hatch. He had helped the yeoman and others up through the same outlet, boosting them with his shoulders. He had joined a gang defusing 500-pound GP, or general-purpose, bombs.

Then he heard Commander Hale, the air officer, order "all aviation personnel off." When someone asked if this included aviation personnel who were a part of the ship's company, it was Groves' understanding that Hale amplified, "I mean *all* aviation personnel get the hell off the ship!"

So, Jack Grove walked off the *Franklin* and onto the *Santa Fe*. As he did so, he reflected on the store of processed cheese he had bought in Hawaii which was still reposing in his locker—not to mention record disks and other items of compelling worth now being abandoned. The men had thought this would be a "long" cruise and quite possibly "pleasant" as well.

Kermit Clingerman, still in a daze, found a blanket to wrap around him. It was windy and the temperature was about 60° F.—not very warm, especially considering the fact that the task force's recent rendezvous point had been in the tropical atmosphere of the Carolinas. The crew's blood had been thinned out.

He would recall:

A group of fellows were manning a hose near the deck edge elevator, which is just forward of the center of the ship, and others were trying to chop holes in the deck with fire axes. A number of fellows were huddled

on the port side of the flight deck, some sitting and
some standing. I went over and sat down.

One of those sitting proved to be a classic case of shell
shock. He had been next to Kermit Clingerman, gesticulat-
ing, moving his lips, but speechless.

"What's wrong?" Clingerman asked. The man could not
reply. Clingerman then summoned one of the corpsmen,
who led the mute sailor across the plank to the *Santa Fe*.

Clingerman watched with an abstract sort of fascination
the line of seamen holding a heavy hawser from the *Santa
Fe*, "to keep the ships as close together as possible, while
banging together and bobbing up and down like a couple of
corks."

It was nearly 11 A.M. when Gehres advised Fitz, "We have
one pump started, shifting fuel to port." Then he added a
postscript: "Can you take us in tow? We have lost all power.
Our towing gear is ready."

It wasn't really ready, however—far from it, in fact.
There was no power in the winches and the anchor chains
were a tangled mess in the fo'c'sle.

Fitz could not handle the tow so he called up the *Pittsburgh*, which was already anticipating just such a request:
"Can you take *Franklin* in tow while we go ahead with personnel and fire fighting?"

Gingrich, on the larger cruiser, did not know how long it
would require to rig for the job or even if Mitscher really
wanted to spare him from the task force screen. His fast
command was not designed as a tugboat, any more than
pilots such as Kilpatrick were supposed to double as firemen.
Ginrickey, nonetheless, did not call back Davison, who had
ordered him to "maneuver in." He simply flashed a "Roger"
to Fitz who at once relayed to Gehres, "We are having *Pittsburgh* come to take you in tow."

The bos'n's whistle piped through the PA system of the

Pittsburgh, followed by the attention-arresting "Rigging party lay aft. Break out the tow . . . !"

Gingrich then ordered flank speed for a few minutes to put the *Pittsburgh* in position well forward of the *Franklin.* He could then adjust astern as needed. The propellers cut a white froth in the sea as the bow of the long cruiser began to inch up out of the water.

To the slanting, littered, and, in some places, hot decks of the *Franklin, Santa Fe* seamen were tossing assorted supplies: medical cases, oxygen rescue breathers, blankets, loaves of bread, even water beakers. Other crewmen from the *Santa Fe* had gone aboard the *Franklin* with new fire hoses and they now began pouring tons of water onto the fires—a tussle which, as Bill Hayler would observe, was "an uphill struggle all the way."

The same officer, lately of the engine room gang, also noted how the port side of the *Santa Fe* was being "chewed up" progressively by the outjuts of the *Franklin's* gallery deck, especially the 40-mm sponsons. Yet, the cruiser stuck, like a faithful dog at his injured master's side.

One sour note, however, sounded in some of those who survived the ordeal. Gehres would report it this way:

> As a result of mistaken generosity on the part of a few junior officers who passed out officers' clothing to enlisted men whose clothing was wet, other men went through the forward officers' quarters and equipped themselves completely in officers' uniforms and insignia of rank.
>
> The appearance of these pseudo-officers on the forecastle and forward end of the flight deck added to the confusion there and undoubtedly was responsible for many men leaving the ship to the *Santa Fe* who should not have done so, but who undoubtedly thought that inasmuch as officers were leaving they should also. . . .

They had every reason to want to put as much distance as

possible between themselves and the *Franklin*. Aside from
the continuing danger from the explosions and the fires, the
men were wet to the skin from tending fire hoses and shiver-
ing in the chill March wind.

Meanwhile, those who had jumped, such as Treadaway,
were swimming or clinging tenaciously to rafts in the deep,
rolling swells. For the most part, they presented a pitiful
sight as they waited to be picked up by destroyers.

Gehres continued:

> This dressing of enlisted men in officers' clothing is
> something which should never be permitted. In this
> case there was an ample supply of heavy protective
> clothing and gas-protective clothing immediately avail-
> able on the forecastle deck, and there was no need for
> any enlisted man to appropriate or wear officers' gear.
>
> On the second approach of the *Santa Fe* to *Franklin* a
> considerable number of uninjured and able-bodied men
> and, sad to relate, a few officers swung over to the *Santa
> Fe* on lines from the forecastle and hangar deck, al-
> though no word was given at any time to abandon ship.

One enlisted man who would quip, "I don't know whether
I had on an ensign's or lieutenant's uniform," held the im-
pression that he had been ordered to go into "officers' country." One man wore a clearly marked admiral's life jacket,
another a commander's coat with the three broad bands.

Others disputed Gehres' assertion that no word had ever
been passed to abandon ship. They swore they never heard
the "Do not," but just "Abandon ship!" Many more would
recall they heard "Stand by to abandon!"

John O'Donovan, the quartermaster, was quite certain
that the order was never officially given. While he would
admit that he was "scared stiff" at least part of the time and
"most anxious to abandon ship," there were other considera-

tions, to his way of thinking, in addition to order and discipline. As he recalled:

> The water directly down from the pilot house was congested with all sorts of litter, crates, logs, all manner of junk, so that to jump from where I was carried a guarantee that I'd get at least a broken leg if not a broken skull. . . . My hopes of surviving were kept flickering by my knowledge that Captain Gehres had given the word for the magazines to be flooded. My memories of what happened to HMS *Hood* [blown up by the *Bismarck* with virtually all hands aboard] a few years earlier and to USS *Princeton* the preceding October were constantly in my mind.

Different members of the *Franklin's* complement reacted to the idea of abandoning ship in their own way, especially those not on the fantail or other areas where explosions made up their minds for them. Seaman Charles I. Smoak of Newington, Georgia, for one, would say of his decision to remain, "There was work to do. My ship was in trouble." Hoyt Williams of Atlanta, would explain that, among other considerations, "I never liked water. It's too cold." So he continued to help jettison ammunition.

Gary, meanwhile, had brought out the final group of trapped men. Dr. Fuelling, pale, begrimed, and exhausted, was among the last. "We'd all be dead," the surgeon gasped, "if it wasn't for Gary. . . ."

The engineer officer, however, was already thinking about other parts of the ship—like his own domain, the evaporator and the rest of the engine spaces. His oxygen breather was almost exhausted. If that bothered him, it did not show.

In a few minutes he was on his way below, once more.

8

CHAPLAIN BELOW

Meanwhile, along with the *Santa Fe* at her side and the *Pittsburgh* maneuvering ahead toward a tow station, the *Franklin* was being driven by a northeast stern wind ever closer to Shikoku, possibly fewer than thirty-eight miles away by this time, shortly after 11 A.M. Navigator Jurika reflected that if the rate of drift were not soon checked, he'd be taking sights on the mountain peaks of that austere Japanese Home Island.

The breeze at least was blowing the smoke to port, so that the starboard side of the carrier was relatively clear. Meanwhile, the sea was sufficiently calm so as not to impair rescue operations.

In the bow, Joe Taylor, led a motley gang of seamen, firemen, cooks, stewards, yeomen—some thirty in all—in hacking away at the starboard anchor with files, steel cutters, cold chisels, and acetylene torches. The plan was to get rid of the anchor, then use the 540 feet of chain as the towline. Anything less sturdy did not impress the exec as sufficiently strong or reliable to haul so mighty a ship.

At 11:28 the *Pittsburgh* advised, perhaps optimistically, that she was "preparing" to take the crippled carrier "in tow."

The fight against the flames continued. When one of the hoses from the *Santa Fe* burst—and in the worst possible place, between the two ships—Seaman George S. Smith of the *Franklin* crawled over the side. Clinging to ropes and to the hose itself, he spliced in a new section. He seemed wholly oblivious to the obvious danger of being crushed between the two ships. Soon, water was flowing through that hose once more.

Simultaneously, electricians were making repairs to an emergency Diesel generator in a forward compartment of the hangar deck. While it remained largely operable, the problem was to splice additional electric cables to it in the hopes of bringing back to life the ship's more important electrical circuits.

While the fire fighting and emergency repairs were going forward, together with efforts to rig a towline and continue transfer of the wounded, there remained priority concerns of rescue. For example, Dr. Fox, with his pharmacists and patients in the hospital bay, hadn't been heard from. And five crewman were still isolated in aft steering.

These concerns were much on O'Callahan's mind as he continued his extra-chaplain's duties here and there on the ship, insisting all the while to himself that it was "stupid to fear death." What bothered him more than anything else was claustrophobia. Even in harbor, he disliked going below into the small compartments: a turret, for example, or a paint locker.

Now, the padre was doing just that. In a 5-inch turret he was helping to pass hot loaded shells outside so they could be jettisoned into the sea. Irrationally, he did not worry as much about the imminent danger of being blown up as he did about being trapped in such a hot, close place. One of the men broke the tension by repeating the line popularized at Pearl Harbor: "Praise the Lord and pass the ammunition!" Then another varied the theme: "Praise the Lord and dump the ammunition!" (The original was attributed to Chaplain Howell Forgy of the cruiser *New Orleans* during the December 7 attack as he exhorted the gunners to load and fire faster.)

Gangs were changed in the turret under Gunnery Officer Bill McKinney, but the chaplain remained until the last bomb was heaved over the side. That did not mean his work was finished.

"Steamship" or "Steamboat" Graham, the good-looking ship's fire marshal, wanted to organize a party to investigate the possibilities of clearing bombs from the gallery deck, ringing the elevations of the burned hangar. Now that the fires in the latter were subsiding, it was possible to venture into these hot, smoking caverns.

O'Callahan had been at Graham's side before. He followed him unhesitatingly again, partly because he did not want Graham to go "alone." As he moved through the wreckage of the carrier, laced everywhere now with a snake pit of hoses, he was beset with questions: "I haven't seen Antonetti, or Rusty Hornbeck. Where is Sheridan, Kasch, Catt, Berger, Morgan, Stein . . . ?" In the men's minds the padre had become a sort of clearing house for missing shipmates. They attributed to him powers none aboard possessed at this time.

The hoses that the chaplain stepped on or sometimes jumped over captured his imagination, "writhing" as they did and "crisscrossing along the deck." He observed the men handling them: "Hose handlers crouch and fall in the blast of another explosion, then get to their feet and grip the hoses again. I saw the look of disgust when a line went dry as another water main ruptured." He watched them ferret out another "riser," link up the hose, and wait expectantly for water—which did not invariably flow.

Graham hesitated before a small door at the portside catwalk located in the gallery passageway, which was beneath the flight deck. It was in the midst of jagged holes along the same bulkhead torn by rockets and bomb splinters. He opened the hatch, to disclose only smoky darkness. There could be floors—"decks"—within. There could also be abysses where there had been decks.

The chaplain asked Graham if he were going on in.

"Yes," the latter replied. He instructed O'Callahan to crawl close behind him on his hands and knees, "but don't push me!"

The two men were engulfed in the blackness. They coughed from the smoke. Water was dripping, somewhere. The passageway was slippery and rough with debris. The chaplain thought, "Could you recognize the devil here even if you touched him?" Surely, it was a very special kind of hell.

Graham's crawl slowed. He halted. The chaplain paused beside his companion. Now that their eyes were becoming accustomed to the murk, shapes and irregularities were appearing in foggy silhouette: stalactite jags of steel, or bulges where bulges shouldn't be.

What had halted Graham, however, were not the hanging steel splinters but the faint outlines of a hole in the metal decking immediately in front of the two. Graham stretched out to his full length, straddled his feet over the hole, and kicked down on the opposite edges.

"We'd better think this over a moment," he said to the chaplain.

Topside, Taylor was racing against time to get that heavy anchor chain out and hook onto the *Pittsburgh* before another plane or planes came in to finish the *Franklin*, which was scarcely better than a sitting duck. The chisels, no matter what the strength and enthusiasm of the wielder, did not make much of a nick in the steel. The torches did. Little by little, the link that held the anchor was burning through.

Gingrich was scarcely happy at the situation of his cruiser, itself perforce almost dead in the water. He had tossed a heavy 8-inch "messenger" over for the *Franklin*. This was a rope eight inches in circumference—which was comparable to a tree branch, its weight greatly magnified by being in the water. With it, the men would haul in a steel towing cable to be fastened to the outboard end of the starboard anchor chain.

Since there was no power on the carrier's capstan, the job was one of muscle power alone. And there was plenty of it, with officers and men thronging the limited bow area. Included were people who had been trapped earlier—Aaron Gill, Henry Willard, Kermit Clingerman, and, briefly, even QM John O'Donovan, who, of course, had never been trapped other than by the demands of his pilot house watch. He marveled at the "enormously heavy cable . . . being hauled aboard by a very large group of men who, straining mightily, would move it only an inch or two on each heave."

They tugged and sweated in the cold air, grunted, gasped, cursed, and tugged some more. Finally, Tom Frasure, who had disputed the term "fried bread" with Chaplain O'Callahan, together with others of the cooks' and stewards' department, hit on an idea. They started chanting an old Negro spiritual with a refrain improvised to answer immediate needs, which went something like: "Yeave—ho! Yeave—ho!"

The response within the bow group was electric. All "yeaved-ho" in rhythm. The huge hawser slackened and then tightened, slackened and tightened. "It was an inspiring sight," Taylor would recall, "to watch the men and officers all pulling together, all chanting."

The wet line did not move a great deal faster, but it kept coming up from the water, over the gunwales, and onto the deck. This would be followed by the steel towing cable itself which would, in turn, be shackled to the *Franklin's* anchor links.

Below, Graham and the chaplain resumed their interrupted crawl. If anything, the passage seemed darker and more smoke-choked. Then, they finally came out at a hatch and obtained the intelligence they had sought. The hangar deck was hot, but not too filled with smoke. The fires were abating. From this position, a hose crew could work on the gallery fires. O'Callahan and Graham inched their way back, obtained a volunteer hose crew, and led the men down the same passage so they could start fighting the fires.

For activity such as this, Jurika would liken the chaplain to someone "doing ten men's work." Joe Taylor found him

a soul-stirring sight. He seemed to be everywhere, giving extreme unction to the dead and dying, urging the men on and himself handling hoses, jettisoning ammunition, and doing everything he could to help save our ship. He was so conspicuous not only because of the Cross dabbed with paint across his helmet, but because of his seemingly detached air as he went from place to place with head slightly bowed as if in meditation or prayer.

Shortly after 12 noon the *Santa Fe* advised the task force, "Captain of the *Franklin* says fires practically under control, skeleton crew aboard, list stabilized at thirteen degrees. If you save us from the Japanese, we will save the ship."

Mitscher replied, "Tell *Franklin* we appreciate his message and will do all we can."

About 12:54, while the *Pittsburgh* was still working on the cable and anchor chain and was almost but not *quite* ready to "take a strain" on the long, complex towline and move ahead, a bogie was picked up from four miles out.

As the "target" dived onto the *Franklin,* it quickly took the shape of another Judy, the same model plane which had already inflicted such punishment.

One bomb started down. Aaron Gill ducked behind a winch, knowing "it was coming for me." In fact, he gripped the winch so hard he was sure he left his imprint on the metallic piece of machinery.

"The bomb looked unreal, several times bigger than the plane that released it!"

But the bomb was not coming for Aaron Gill, nor, as it turned out, for the carrier. It passed 200 yards to starboard, hit the water, detonated in a geyser, and shook the ship.

In seconds the Judy was "splashed" by the concentrated fire from the task force, including the few 40-mm guns of the *Franklin* still operable. The "superbly active" (as O'Donovan thought of it) combat air patrol from the task force shot down another Judy before it came close to the *Franklin*.

The gun crews were now a motley assortment: yeomen, laundrymen, two buglers from the band, even the captain's Marine orderly, Wallace Klimkiewiez from Jersey City. But they were badly needed since many of the regular gunners had been killed.

By now the anchor had been cut through and dropped and the steel cable had been attached to the anchor chain. Between 1 and 2 P.M. several false starts were made in towing. Listing as she was, the heavy vessel tended to move at right angles. This condition was somewhat improved by having Brookie Davis and the others trapped in the steering compartment change the position of the rudder with hand gear and tackle.

However, the *Franklin* was soon making three knots—scarcely fast, but better than drifting toward Japan, as she had been.

9

"WHAT THE HELL HAPPENED?"

Meanwhile, there were those in the water awaiting rescue.

Budd Faught had successfully eluded the turbulent wash of the carrier. He rode up and down the big propeller wave but fortunately was not drawn below.

He had no life jacket since his was still in the shattered ready room, and his suit had not inflated in spite of the efforts of his squadron leader to blow it up. In fact, the latter, Marine Captain Jones, had not survived that last explosion which Faught had barely missed.

The water was "pretty cold," though not as bad as Faught thought it would be. His broken legs were useless, floating out behind him, but he paddled with his one unbroken arm to keep his head up.

There were others in the water all around him, some drowning, and there was nothing he could do about it. In a few minutes a seat cushion from one of the aircraft floated along and he grabbed hold of it. That was a help. Then, a can of some sort bumped into him, which he pushed off.

Drenched and blinded by the water, he soon looked up to see the *Franklin*, which had gone away, coming back toward him, "towering like a house." For a moment he was fearful that it would run him down. Listing, smoking, exploding, the stricken carrier passed, its wash again tumbling him about.

Then he came up on a raftlike affair of cargo nets and floats filled with sailors, some clutching to the far edges. A few of the men were shouting and altogether the scene seemed to be one of panic.

The pilot decided he was better off by himself on the cushion under his good arm, even though he was now very much alone in the Pacific. This seemed strange considering the size of the task force.

Time passed. His legs remained numb. He became conscious of people singing and wondered where he was. Soon he recognized the tune: "Give me land, lots of land . . . don't fence me in . . . !"

Riding up and down over the swells was a bunch of survivors in a rubber life raft, making some progress by means of paddling. They kept on, not noticing Budd Faught, or not caring to. Presently they were gone, wraithlike and unreal as they had come, and the singing faded.

He floated on in a timeless haze until a slow-moving destroyer loomed ahead. It hauled up so close that he was able to hook his arm into a chain hanging from the bow.

But he still had not been noticed. As the vessel dipped up and down, Faught went with it, barely able to inhale a deep breath in anticipation of the next ducking. He yelled and shouted.

Finally, a seaman peered over the side at him and called, "Climb on up!"

"I can't," Faught replied, spitting out water. "Both my legs and an arm are broken."

The sailor did not seem to fully comprehend Faught's plight. At least his response was very slow. While he was figuratively scratching his head, a life raft approached laden with men who appeared to be clad only in long underwear.

Another face appeared above the injured pilot, then came

a shout: "Here! Get this rope around you. We'll haul you up."

Budd managed to catch the rope and twine it around his body. But before he could be pulled up, a strange thing happened. The underwear-clad sailors all began moving up the side to the rope over Faught's body. He had to wait until the last foot was off his shoulders before it was his turn to be brought onto the destroyer. It proved to be the *Marshall* and "Boy, was I glad to see her!"

The destroyer already had 211 survivors aboard.

Faught was taken to the wardroom where he was given seven pints of blood by concerned hospital corpsmen. Both legs were then placed in a cast, and he was transferred, for greater comfort, to the captain's bunk.

Others were being picked up, too, this early afternoon, including Roy Treadaway of the after auxiliary machine room. He was rescued by the *Miller*, which had taken Admiral Davison off the *Franklin*. Norman Titus, the pharmacist mate who jumped off the fantail, was fished out by the destroyer *Hunt*, which had rescued nearly fifty men, about the same number as the *Miller*.

The *Santa Fe*, with 832 officers and men from the *Franklin*, carried the record number. About 100 of these were casualties. Her medical staff would operate and tend to burns for the next forty-eight hours without cessation.

Joe Lafferty, who finally had been taken aboard the *Santa Fe*, was found to have suffered a compound fracture of his right foot in addition to burns and cuts. Ahead for him lay the hospital ship, *Relief*, a base hospital at Guam, and many months on crutches. Yet he would ultimately make a complete recovery without scars, "thanks to the good medical attention I received."

He would also concede, "It is a miracle to be alive when a 500-pound bomb blew up at your feet!"

At 3:45 P.M. the *Franklin* was being towed away from the Japanese islands at seven knots, closely protected by the faithful though battered *Santa Fe*. The *Pittsburgh*, though she had firepower, was in no condition to maneuver.

It was now time for stock-taking, licking wounds, and counting losses. The totals were, at the very least, sobering: 832 dead and nearly 300 wounded—one-third of the crew. No ship in history had been ravaged by such losses and yet remained afloat. Only 704 remained aboard to manage the huge carrier: 600 men and 103 officers plus Gehres. At muster only 250 of these men and 75 officers could report "fit for duty" in the literal sense.

And the ship was still a mess. Jurika described the situation:

> The deck was a mad shambles of burned, warped, and broken wood and steel, with bodies, debris, and wreckage littering the area. Holes were cut in the flight deck with axes, and hoses were poked through in an attempt to quell flames still raging on the gallery deck.

It seemed to Gehres that the "major explosions" were now past, "although there were sporadic explosions of 40-mm and smaller stuff."

In addition:

> The list was steadied at an average thirteen degrees to starboard, the ship down about three feet by the stern, and the fires on the forward end of the hangar deck extinguished and those in the after part of the hangar deck, in the gallery deck, and in other parts of the ship were gradually being brought under control.

Gehres found that the only fire main pressure remaining was in the two Diesel emergency fire pumps in the fo'c'sle.

Enemy aircraft, meanwhile, were still trying to finish off the *Franklin*. But the Japanese planes could not make it through the wall of AA fire from the task force or the fighter umbrella from the other carriers.

There was an exception or two. Lt. Cdr. David Berger, a lawyer from Philadelphia, would recall that he "looked for foxholes" every time he saw an unidentified aircraft: "We dug our noses in the deck all right." Once, when it seemed that the plane was strafing, "chewing up the deck," he ducked behind a 5-inch gun mount. When he suddenly realized that the gun as well as the magazine was smoking "like the very devil," he decided that was a very poor hiding place.

The afternoon moved toward evening. Dusk was nearing, which meant that the last fires had to be extinguished if the *Franklin* were not to become a beacon for the Japanese. Weary hose parties kept at their tasks.

Makeshift sick bays—Dr. Fox, his pharmacists, and patients were still unreported in the hospital ward—were crowded. The remaining surgeons—Fuelling, Smith, and Sherman—worked heroically on the burned and wounded who for one reason or another had not been transferred. Chaplain Gatlin had himself become adept in handling morphine injections as well as in wound sterilization and bandaging.

All in all, especially with the ship moving again, things were looking up. In fact, Jurika later observed:

> When, generally by officer messengers, word finally reached the bridge of the condition of the *Franklin*, our outlook seemed quite hopeful. The engineer officer was called to investigate the condition of the engines and firerooms, and later reported that as soon as the spaces cooled sufficiently to permit habitability the machinery could probably be coaxed into action. An investigation was begun on the condition of all accessible spaces.

Now, at long last, the men could think about necessities which had been forgotten during the long, nightmare day— like eating and washing up. There wasn't much variety of food available and virtually no water to moisten throats that had remained dry from tension and apprehension. However, canned pork sausage and orange juice finally arrived on the bridge—a "gourmet's delight" in Jurika's appraisal. "Best damn meal I ever tasted!" seconded Taylor, the exec.

At 1813—thirteen minutes past 6 P.M.—the quartermaster logged, "Ship darkened except for small glow from fire, frame 200."

The *Santa Fe* and several destroyers hovered nearby in case their help in fighting the remaining fires was needed.

It was past time to attempt to rescue Brookie Davis and his companions still trapped in steering aft. Lt. (jg) E. Robert "Bob" Wassman of New York, twenty-four-year-old assistant navigating officer, volunteered to lead a rescue party in the attempt. Captain Gehres phoned Davis the welcome news that they were trying to break through.

It wasn't easy. Wassman steered his group aft through the wreckage of the flight deck. On the port side it was all but impossible to find a ladder leading below, for whole sections had been blown off. Ladders on the starboard were badly twisted, but usable.

"Above the sloshing water," Wassman would recall, "we worked our way over the hot and twisted metal to the fantail. I heard a boy moaning and after a search found him badly hurt lying among a group of dead." One of the party picked him up and carried him back out.

With rescue breathers and flashlights, they inched down. They passed a bone-tired hose party washing away gasoline where it spurted along a passageway. They stumbled over debris, made wrong turnings, arriving at deadends. Ultimately, they reached the compartment directly above that occupied by the five trapped men. The water inside was almost waist-deep. If they found a hatch and opened it, they would incur the risk of drowning those below.

Accordingly, Wassman took his volunteers through the torturous passages topside again for hand pumps. They returned as speedily as the route and their weariness permitted and started pumping.

When the compartment contained less than a foot of water, a message was tapped to Davis. The rescuers had located a hatch and were about to open it.

They did. The five below were soaked, but they didn't care. They had been freed.

When Brookie Davis finally was led onto the deck and surveyed the nightmare scene, he was momentarily speechless. Then he asked, "What the hell happened?"

They had been imprisoned for some seventeen hours. It was nearly midnight.

And so ended for all those remaining aboard the *Franklin* the longest day of their lives.

10

"OLD BIG BEN, SHE AIN'T WHAT SHE USED TO BE..."

As the *Franklin* struggled through the night, a Pacific Fleet communique from Guam announced obliquely, "Carrier aircraft of the Pacific Fleet continued their attacks on Japan on March 19. They attacked Kobe, Kure, and other objectives in and around the Inland Sea."

The New York Times correspondent somewhat amplified the story:

> Pacific Fleet carrier planes that had attacked the Southern Empire Island of Kyushu on Sunday swept northward yesterday to blast Japanese objectives at Kobe, Japan's principal port, and Kure, the most important naval base of the Empire. Both cities are on Honshu, main island of the enemy homeland.

Meanwhile, Tommy Greene and other engineering officers, including Don Gary, had returned with their men into the suffocating heat of the engine and fire rooms. Shortly before midnight fires were sparked into life beneath Boiler No. 5. An hour and a half later, steam was up and No. 3 generator was running. One by one, the other boilers were lit.

But it was a long process to coax the boilers up to super-heat—1,200 PSI—so that there would be sufficient steam to spin the big turbines. Sweating, weary beyond description, the engineers worked on.

As they did so, their rooms and those of the other officers, located in the forward section of the ship, were turned over to the enlistees and noncommissioned officers, most of whose fo'c'sles aft had been burned or otherwise damaged. Two or three to a bunk, the men piled in for whatever sleep they could obtain.

Topside, the fires were not altogether out. While the *Franklin* was not quite "lit up like a carnival," as Bill Hayler observed, or even "a flaming beacon," in Father O'Callahan's description, there were sufficient sporadic blazes—as the gasoline reservoirs burned slowly into exhaustion—to keep fire fighters busy. Gehres wrote, "Fires broke out in various parts of the ship, including the flight deck, and the fire parties were hampered by darkness and the indescribable wreckage. They had their hands full all night."

Twice, destroyers from the screen steamed alongside with all hoses pumping to assist. The *Miller* drew up at 8 o'clock, a few hours later joined by the destroyer *Bullard*, to pump water onto the fantail against a particularly stubborn fire.

One seaman aboard the *Franklin*, directing the destroyers' hoses from a dangerous perch on a jagged outthrust strip of metal, was unable to regain the deck for several hours, unwilling to move any more than he had to in the dark.

There were additional concerns, as the captain continued:

> Steering was very difficult because due to the heavy starboard list, *Franklin* persisted in sheering up to port and sailing to windward, dragging the *Pittsburgh's* stern around.
>
> At about 2200, counterflooding operations to reduce the list were commenced. As damage control was inac-

cessible and the hydraulic controls of the counterflooding valves were out of commission, officers and men had to make their way below on the portside forward with rescue breathers to find and open the valves to flood the forward port voids. Their instructions were to reduce the list to about five degrees to starboard and hold it there, as the ship was heavily flooded both below decks and in the gallery decks, with a great deal of free water surface.

Counterflooding operations got out of control, however, and at about 0200 the ship rolled to port and stayed there with a list of about ten degrees. No further counterflooding operations of any kind were permitted after that.

Dawn revealed a most welcome sight: the battle cruisers *Guam* and *Alaska* steaming over the horizon to join an escort which already included the *Santa Fe*, the tow ship *Pittsburgh*, and four destroyers.

As a matter of fact, Budd Faught was now aboard the *Alaska*, having been transferred from the *Marshall* in a wire basket. He had been overlooked briefly, resting atop a 5-inch gun mount, which was blazing away furiously at enemy planes.

By now, the Marine aviator had already heard the bad news: he would have to lose his left leg below the knee. The break had arrested circulation and the long immersion in cold water had sealed the limb's doom. At that, Budd considered himself lucky, since an experienced orthopedic surgeon was numbered among the big ship's medical staff.

On the *Franklin* the hundreds of dead posed far more of a problem than the living. Many were buried beneath I-beams, steel netting, twisted catwalks, and other metal debris warped into every grotesque shape and all but defying easy removal. It could require an hour or more of herculean effort to recover just one deceased shipmate.

Chaplains O'Callahan and Gatlin waited on the quarter deck for the remains to be brought up on stretchers. For obvious sanitary reasons they had to be consigned to the deep with the utmost speed. Even had there been sufficient pharmacist personnel available, embalming or even wrapping was not indicated.

There was time only for a brief prayer from one of the chaplains before another Navy man went to rest in the sea: a type of burial historically sought by the seafarer.

Sometimes O'Callahan himself went below to aid in the gruesome task. Once, he would recall, he fell sound asleep, utterly exhausted, halfway down a ladder.

One man, at least, was found alive more than twenty-four hours after the attack. Badly burned and in shock, he insisted that he had been at the barber's getting a haircut. But why would anyone have his hair trimmed at that hour and in combat conditions?

He was turned over to Dr. Fuelling while another search party sloshed through littered water trying to find the compartment where the injured one claimed he had obtained that haircut. The quest was abortive.

The physical wreckage was challenge enough for removal: parts of planes, shattered guns and gun mounts, stanchions, beams, ventilators, even the "Beast," the huge hangar deck crane used to pick up wrecked aircraft. However, a lucky find—four intact jeeps—aided the crew immensely in the job of clearing. Soon wreckage was being dumped overboard at an ever-accelerating rate, like some mammoth spring housecleaning.

Four boilers were now "on the line" and Gehres asked permission to cast loose his tow, asserting he could make fifteen knots. About 12:30 this Tuesday, March 20, the *Franklin*, once more a ship steaming on her own, though heavily shepherded, set course for Ulithi.

Lt. "Steamship" Graham arrived at the pilot house and

reported, in O'Donovan's hearing, that he had finally gotten into the magazines.

"They were flooded, weren t they?" asked Gehres.

"Bone dry," replied Graham.

"My God," murmured the captain, who, O'Donovan claimed, "proceeded to turn an interesting shade of green and purple."

In other words, if the fires had gone a little lower, the whole carrier would have been blown to bits.

The enemy had not forgotten the *Franklin*. At 2:30 P.M. a Judy, the same type that had dealt the carrier so crippling a blow, eluded the fighter screen and the escort's flak to make a fast glide bombing run out of the sun. The plane swooped in from the starboard bow to be taken immediately under 40-mm fire from a volunteer crew. The pilot pulled up and swerved as he dropped his bomb.

It caught O'Donovan as well as Chaplain O'Callahan in the flag bridge, from which vantage point they watched with fascination the falling bomb. It crossed the flight deck, barely missing the port deck edge, and exploded in the water about 200 feet off the port quarter, shaking but not seriously harming the *Franklin*.

Two hours later another bogey was splashed by Navy planes forty-eight miles from its objective.

Still later in the afternoon the Catholic chaplain was crossing the flight deck when a plane suddenly materialized to start a strafing run.

He would recount:

> I should have crouched to the deck to make myself as small a target as possible. I didn't crouch, but not from bravado or fearlessness. The effort involved in having to climb to my feet again seemed just then to be a greater evil than any number of bullets that might be splashing around.

He wondered if one, after all, could become "sated" with the presence of danger. He also 'resented" the intrusion of the Japanese while he was still concerned with burying the dead.

That evening a precious bit of cargo was found: cases of beer. Gehres ordered it distributed to the crew. Unofficially, there was also the chaplain's and the surgeons' stores of stronger beverage. These, added to what the pilots were forced to leave behind, proved ample morale builders.

There still was not much food: a few slices of bread, bacon, fat, Spam, and some fruit juice. However, the stewards were continuing to batter through the debris to emergency stores, while the escort ships were preparing to make transfers from their own larders.

At 6 P.M. Fitz had logged on the *Santa Fe*: "Today the *Franklin* cast off its tow. I have just received a report that she is able to make twenty-one knots. We have come 207 miles from where the *Franklin* was hit, but we are still only 225 miles from places where the Jap airfields are located."

Perhaps Hal Fitz had exaggerated the ship's speed, but only slightly. Gehres himself would report:

> During that night, *Franklin* worked up to eighteen knots, course 135° [true]. Flares and firing could be seen during the first and mid-watches on the horizon astern, where groups of enemy aircraft encountered other task groups, where they apparently expected to find the helpless *Franklin*.
>
> By this time the ship had four boilers steaming, the after two engines operating normally and auxiliary steam from the after plant passing through the turbogenerator cross-connection going into the forward engines, thus obtaining some thrust instead of a dead drag from the outboard propellers.

What Gehres was reporting was that since No. 2 fire room

had been made inoperative by the first blast, steam had to be moved from the after boilers forward to drive the turbines hooked up to the now dead boilers. This involved a laborious opening and closing of valves in order that the steam would arrive at its proper destination—the turbines, and not the dead boilers.

Most of the ventilation was now back in the engine spaces. A gyro compass was working again and the broken antenna to the search radar had been repaired.

The majority of the fires were out, although a few still flickered on the gallery deck, the captain's cabin, and in some of the lower spaces toward the stern.

Also the carrier now boasted three distinct gun positions in operation—5-inch and 40-mm forward and another 40-mm on the bridge. A sound-powered telephone system had been jury-rigged from the bridge to these batteries.

By short-range radio, messages of congratulation began to arrive that night. From Admiral Mitscher:

> You and your historic crew cannot be too highly applauded for your historic and successful battle to save your gallant ship, in spite of the difficulty, the enormity of which is appreciated. Deep regrets for your losses which we feel as our own.

And from the *Franklin's* erstwhile admiral, Davison:

> Congratulations. I may be on a stranger's doorstep now but I claim you again with pride. Battered though you may be you are still my child. Great work.

He was joined by Fitz of the *Santa Fe*:

> Congratulations on heroic work and outstanding efficiency of yourself and men in getting underway and saving her. It is an example we will never forget.

And so the messages poured in, from all levels of command, from carrier division commanders down to individual captains of destroyers. A few even retained some capacity for humor, as, for example, one observed: "To you and your great gang we touch our scorched forelocks!"

Gehres replied to each briefly:

> My ship's company and I thank you for your message and for the protection received in our worst hours.

Wednesday, the 21st, two days after the attack, was much like the preceding day—searching, clearing away wreckage, and the dreary, continuing burials. The carrier was still in range of land-based Japanese aircraft, and two tried to attack at noon. The first was shot down by escort planes in sight of the carrier, exploding violently in the water and sending up a huge geyser. The second was destroyed over the horizon.

Curiously, as Gehres logged, "hot fires" still burned in the gallery deck and in the commanding officer's cabin country.

It was time, Joe Taylor, the executive officer, decided, to think about morale and the smartness of the ship even though, through force of circumstances, it probably could not be described as a "taut ship." He found a mimeograph machine and banged out a plan for the coming day, the 22d, headed:

BIG BEN BOMBED, BATTERED, BRUISED AND
BENT BUT NOT BROKEN.

The plan then read:

> 1. All hands wear clean dungarees, blue-dyed hats, black shoes to quarters. Chins up, chests out, tails over the dashboard.
>
> 2. Gun crews will wear helmets. All usable gun batteries will be manned.

During the night the last fires were doused. Thursday, in their clean dungarees, just as the order had it, and, for the most part, chins up, the men were back to work at the seemingly endless task of cleaning up the ship and still seeking dead bodies. In some areas the familiar salty sound of the chipping hammer was heard, preparatory to the wielding of paintbrushes. There were those, in fact, who would complain that Gehres had put the refurbishing of his own quarters too high on the list of priorities. Yet both Gehres and Taylor knew that it was good to keep the men busy and their thoughts off themselves.

That day the *Franklin* rendezvoused in "Fueling Area Bedbug" with Task Force 58. In midafternoon, escorted by the faithful *Santa Fe*, the carriers *Wasp* and *Enterprise*, and destroyers, she set course for Ulithi, making about twenty knots.

In the evening, after the crew's first hot meal since the attack, Taylor posted his Friday orders, under the heading "A Ship That Won't be Sunk Can't be Sunk":

> 1. Due to our after gasoline system being damaged, smoking regulations must be strictly enforced. You may smoke on the forecastle during the daylight hours. You may smoke in the forward messing compartment between reveille and taps. Officers may smoke in the wardroom. Never throw a lighted butt over the side.
>
> 2. Keep busy doing something all the time. If you aren't on a scheduled working party, work anyway. We've got the world by the tail, hang on.
>
> 3. Do not throw any usable article over the side. If you think it can be salvaged, stack it neatly on the hangar deck just forward of No. 3 elevator on the starboard side.
>
> 4. Anyone knowing the whereabouts of any musical instruments report to the chaplain.

5. Any personal effects such as wallets, watches, etc., shall be turned in to the Executive Officer's cabin.

Item 4 became a special challenge. Except for two trumpets, a guitar, an ocarina, and a clarinet, all the band instruments, including drums, had been destroyed. But Bandmaster Saxie Dowell and his men were innovative. Galley tubs, it was discovered, made excellent base drums when covered tightly with tarpaulins. Fire buckets and pans served as smaller drums and cymbals, with spoons for drumsticks. A jug doubled as a bull fiddle. A penny whistle or two completed the newly-instrumented ship's band.

Early Saturday afternoon the *Franklin* steamed into Ulithi Lagoon. The band, with its unusual assortment of instruments, was lined up on the blackened, pocked flight deck. It struck up, with a raucous, tinny sound and some inevitable discord, the tune of "The Old Gray Mare." But the chorus was quite something else:

Oh, the Old Big Ben, she ain't what she used to be,
Ain't what she used to be, just a few days ago. . . .
Bombs in the hangar deck . . . !

This was followed by a crashing of spoons and hammers against the galley tubs.

The bandsmen soon were joined by others of the crew. The words echoed across the lagoon in this somewhat unorthodox entry of a major warship into port. But then, there was nothing especially orthodox in what the *Franklin* had been through.

11

THE FRANKLIN
COMES HOME

As rain fell fitfully Sunday, a mass as well as a Protestant service of Thanksgiving was held on the flight deck.

Prayed the Reverend Gatlin:

> And since it is of Thy mercy, O gracious Father, that another week is added to our lives, we here dedicate again our souls and our bodies to Thee and Thy service, in a sober, righteous and Godly life; during the week we made new resolutions and in these, do Thou, O merciful God confirm and strengthen us; that, as we grow in age we may grow in grace, and in the knowledge of our Lord and Saviour Jesus Christ who taught us to pray.

The services closed with the Navy Hymn:

> Eternal Father, strong to save,
> Whose arm doth bind the restless wave,
> Who bid'st the mighty ocean deep,
> Its own appointed limits keep;
> O hear us when we cry to Thee
> For those in peril on the sea. . . .

These solemnities were followed by memorial services for the dead, conducted within the ruin of the hangar deck and concluding with volleys from a Marine firing squad.

It was at Ulithi that, with the help of equipment from other ships, the after portions of the *Franklin* were finally pumped out, making it possible to get through to sick bay. The door was broken down to disclose the bodies of Dr. Fox, his seven pharmacist mates, and several patients, lying in a few inches of water. They had not drowned—but suffocated.

The flooded passageways, a result of the fire fighting, had trapped the men in sick bay. Unlike Dr. Fuelling and a few patients such as Joe Gruttadauria who had quickly gotten out of sick bay, Dr. Fox and the others had waited too long. The surgeon and his pharmacist mates had been unwilling to leave their patients, some of whom could not be moved.

Monday evening the hospital ship *Bountiful* sent an entertainment group over to the carrier. The blackened hangar deck wasn't much of a theater, but it had to serve.

During these three days some salvageable material, including bombs and airplane parts, was transferred ashore for future use. A searching party discovered one Tiny Tim wedged dangerously in a hole in the second deck and looking as though it might go off at any moment. It was tugged loose, carried topside by volunteers, then lowered carefully into the water.

On Tuesday, March 27, it was time to continue eastward for Hawaii. At sunset the *Franklin* was under way, preceded by the *Santa Fe*, which logged:

The *Santa Fe* steamed toward Mugai Channel with "Homeward Bound" pennant streamed aft, dipping in the ship's wake 100 yards astern. This was the moment all men and officers had been waiting for the last six months. This is to be *Santa Fe*'s first period and her crew's first leave period since commissioning on 24 November 1942. At 1836 passed through Point Able headed eastward.

The departure was accompanied by a letter from Admiral Raymond A. Spruance, commander of the Fifth Fleet: "The courage, fortitude and ability of you and your crew in saving and bringing back *Franklin* for future use against the enemy cannot be too highly praised."

Wednesday afternoon, the band, still with its makeshift instruments, gave a short concert. Those crew members who could perform magic tricks or were otherwise theatrically inclined put on an impromptu show. Gehres himself addressed the audience: "We are going to take this ship back out and get even with the little yellow scoundrels. I for one am going to be the first volunteer to take her back."

There was not much jollity, however. The shrunken crew was still busy cleaning up the ship, shoveling debris including huge quantities of water-soaked swollen beans. There was, too, a major item of inventory: the personal effects of some 2,000 officers and men, not alone those of the dead but those who had left the ship, including the aviators. But at least the *Franklin* was out of the danger zone.

One month to the day since she had put Diamond Head astern, the *Franklin* sailed into Pearl Harbor. She steamed through the narrow channel opposite Fort Kamehameha, which the enemy had tried so desperately to block on December 7 . . . on past the hospital and the administration building. She made a large sweeping turn toward the dock.

There, lined up, smart in their light blue uniforms, was a glee club of WAVES preparing to welcome the carrier back with the traditional *Aloha*.

Normally, when a ship returns ceremoniously, all hands are mustered at "quarters for entering port." On a carrier perhaps as many as two-thirds of the complement of 3,000 would be mustered in best dress uniforms on the flight deck at attention—a most impressive spectacle. But the *Franklin* numbered her crew not in the thousands but in the hundreds and she had precious little flight deck left. Some 400 who could be spared from their duties were mustered forward on the flight deck, the only section where they could stand.

The WAVES broke into song, clear yet soft and feminine, as the carrier drew closer in. Then the girls looked more closely. Through the torn hatches they could peer into the scorched and somber hangar deck. It was obvious to anyone the ordeal the ship had endured.

One by one, their voices faltered, then, as it seemed to Father O'Callahan, "melted away" altogether into silence. It was obvious from their expressions that some of the WAVES had already begun to cry.

Saxie Dowell and his men, however, were ready. They struck up as they had on the entrance into Ulithi: "Oh, the Old Big Ben, she ain't what she used to be . . . !"

It was picked up by the men mustered on deck, next by some of those on the dock, even those WAVES who had recovered their composure.

Mooring lines were tossed. In moments the *Franklin* was docked at Pearl.

But she remained there only a few days. There were no facilities for the sort of repairs the carrier needed. Men went ashore, where some received mail, thanks to the remarkable means by which the armed forces postal people kept track of ships and men. The chaplain discovered that his sister, Rose Marie, a Maryknoll nun, was alive in Manila.

There was little celebration, however, in sailor haunts in Honolulu. The men seemingly were still too stunned from "the grisly events of March 19," as O'Donovan rationalized it.

Veteran shipyard workers shook their heads and some even went so far as to suggest that she could never make it back to the States. The *Franklin* nonetheless put out to sea. Destination: New York.

"We took," recalled John O'Donovan, "a leisurely nineteen days' cruise from Hawaii to the Canal Zone, beautiful weather all the way, sunbathing on the flight deck every day, a completely enjoyable ocean voyage. I feel that this repaired our nerves. At Panama City one watch went ashore. At Colon the other watch went ashore."

And this time the men did live it up.

Before the carrier cleared the canal, a life raft was accidentally tripped, hitting a tug named *Diablo*. Off the Florida coast there was a submarine contact reported by her destroyer escort. At about the same time, April 12, flags were half-staffed: the President and Commander-in-Chief, Franklin D. Roosevelt, had died.

On April 26, at 2:23 P.M., a cool and windy Thursday five weeks after the attack, the *Franklin* dropped anchor in Gravesend Bay at the approaches to New York Harbor, having completed a voyage of some 12,000 miles. Two days later she warped alongside Pier 12 at the New York Navy Yard in Brooklyn.

"Big Ben" had come home.

POSTSCRIPT

Never in the history of the United States Navy had so many medals and commendations been bestowed on a crew as the result of one action.

There were two Medals of Honor, a record in itself: to Chaplain O'Callahan and to Donald Gary. The accompanying citation for the padre commenced:

> For conspicuous gallantry and intrepidity at the risk of his life above and beyond the call of duty . . . a valiant and forceful leader, calmly braving the perilous barriers of flame and twisted metal to aid his men and his ship, Lieutenant Commander O'Callahan groped his way through smoke-filled corridors to the flight deck and into the midst of violently exploding bombs, shells, rockets and other armament. With the ship rocked by incessant explosions, with debris and fragments raining down and fires raging in ever-increasing fury, he ministered to the wounded and dying, comforting and encouraging men of all faiths. . . .

Gary's citation noted in part:

Staunchly determined, he struggled back to the messing compartment three times despite menacing flames, flooding water and the ominous threat of sudden additional explosions . . . an inspiring and courageous leader, Lieutenant Gary rendered self-sacrificing service under the most perilous conditions and by his heroic initiative, fortitude and valor was responsible for the saving of several hundred lives.

A total of nineteen Navy Crosses were awarded, including one to Captain Gehres:

He displayed outstanding resourcefulness in directing the measures which eventually brought the fires under control, got power back to his ship and enabled her to be withdrawn from a position close aboard a hostile coast.

One went to Gehres' executive officer, Joe Taylor:

With utmost disregard for his personal safety, he visited all sections of the badly damaged ship, leading, inspiring the crew in the gallant and successful effort to salvage the drifting and erupting carrier. In the face of further enemy attacks and explosions of the carrier's own arms he took charge of the towing operations which resulted in getting his ship underway.

Other Navy Crosses went to Commander Hale, the air officer; to Jurika, the navigator; Dr. Fuelling; Dr. Smith; Dr. Fox (posthumously); Dr. Sam Sherman; to Tommy Greene, the engineering officer; to McKinney, the gunnery officer; to Mac Kilpatrick; Lindsey "Red" Morgan; and others.

Silver Star Medals went to twenty-two, including Chaplain Gatlin, Commander Berger, Steamship Graham, Bob

Wassman, who rescued those trapped in steering aft, and Holbrook "Brookie" Davis, among those rescued.

There were 115 Bronze Star Medals including those to George Cheney, in CIC, Ensign Jortberg, and Benjamin Durrance (posthumously), who had tried to save those in sick bay, and to Marine Private Wallace Klimkiewiez, who helped reman a gun.

There were 234 Letters of Commendation including those to "Wild Bill" Hayler, to Quartermaster O'Donovan, Kermit Clingerman, and Henry Willard.

SPECIAL APPENDIX

Other ships have seemingly defied all natural and physical laws of survival to limp home in ruined and sinking condition, following combat.

Examples unquestionably predate properly recorded history, when man first made use of the waters as an avenue of trade, and of combat. To confine these recollections to the United States, however, the first such incident which comes to mind involves the encounter between the American brig *Enterprise* and the British brig *Boxer* in the War of 1812.

The action took place on September 5, 1813, nine miles west of Monhegan Island or some thirty miles east of Portland, Maine. The ships were quite even, the *Enterprise* being of 221 tons, the *Boxer*, 181; the former with a crew of 102 and mounting fourteen "big guns," or 18-pounders; the latter with seventy-four aboard and mounting twelve comparable cannon.

The captains, twenty-eight-year-old William Burrows of the *Enterprise*, and Samuel Blyth of the *Boxer*, only two years his senior, opened up with close-range broadsides in a curious midafternoon engagement which was to see both captains mortally wounded by musket balls and their commands turned into shambles within a few minutes. The two brigs were disabled, with sails, yards, and tackle strewing over the decks. The *Boxer* was holed many times at the waterline.

"Don't give up the ship!" the dying Burrows implored his second-in-command, Lt. Edward R. McCall. "We'll take her yet!"

The report conveyed to McCall from the carpenter was that the *Enterprise* had "suffered much in spars and rigging," and he did not see how the vessel could be maneuvered further. Thus, there was sentiment aboard for surrender.

Crewmen of that mind, however, did not realize how much more the *Boxer* herself had "suffered." In fact, when McCall, without much conviction, called on the Britisher to surrender, the surprising word was returned that she *had*. The problem was: her colors had been nailed to a mast stub and it would take a few minutes to unfasten them. It was 4 P.M., just forty-five minutes after the first crashing broadsides.

Gallantly, Burrows, who still breathed, refused the dead Blyth's sword when it was brought aboard. Instead, he ordered McCall to see that his adversary's widow got it.

Both ships were patched up and the pumps put into operation on the *Boxer*. Late that autumn night the victor and vanquished limped into Casco Bay, the enemy man-of-war wallowing low. Neither brig, by all the sine qua nons of naval architecture and watertight integrity, should really have made it to port. But both did.

In the irony of life and warfare, the captains were buried side by side on a high bluff—Eastern Promenade in Portland—overlooking the sea and the distant arena of their last battle. Their remains are there still, beneath a weathered marker.

The Civil War "at sea" was intense at times, but it was fought along the East Coast, the Gulf of Mexico, in bays and along rivers. Confederate land batteries were a common and sometimes formidable opponent of the Union Navy. If a ship wasn't sunk outright, its chances of making port or being beached were eminently good.

A notable exception was the duel in the English Channel between the Confederate *Alabama* and the powerful Union sloop *Kearsarge* on June 19, 1864. The famed Southern raider, which had captured or sunk seventy vessels, would have desired to return to the sanctuary of neutral Cherbourg, but she never did. With fires out, she sank within seven miles of the harbor breakwater.

Numerous ships struggled homeward during World War I in spite of seemingly mortal damage. Classic examples after the Battle of Jutland, May 31, 1916, were the German battle cruiser *Seydlitz*, which barely made it back to Wilhelmshaven, burdened with more than 5,000 tons of water cascading through her many shell holes, grounding several times on reefs; and the badly-mauled British battleships *Marlborough* and *Warspite*.

In October 1917 America's first year of the Great War, the gun crew of the 5,000-ton U.S.-flag *J. L. Luckenbach* fought it out with the *U-62* for two crackling hours. The big freighter was aflame and shipping water.

"Her captain," wrote Ernst Hashagen, the submarine commander, "defends her cargo with courage and tenacity . . . a brisk and lively fight in which one can see the enemy and set about him. She seems to have suffered in the action but is holding and reports, 'still afloat and fighting!' "

Finally the USS *Nicholson*, a four-stack destroyer, arrived on the scene and scored a hit on the *U-62*. The battle was over as the submarine submerged.

The fires on the *Luckenbach* were extinguished, the

pumps started, the wounded treated by the *Nicholson's* assistant surgeon. Listing sharply, she steamed the 300 miles from the Scilly Isles, off which the battle had commenced, to Le Havre.

The *SC-28*, a 110-foot subchaser, one of a sizable "splinter fleet," "mosquitos," or "Cinderellas," which had sprung into being in a few months, experienced engine trouble en route to the Azores. Sails were rigged by her French crew from blankets, bedsheets, and tablecloths. Other linen was stuffed in leaking seams. Averaging about two knots, tacking this way and that, *SC-28* finally arrived in Fayal, the Azores— one month after her breakdown.

Her crewmen were bronzed, emaciated, down to rainwater and bread crusts. But they were alive. They had saved themselves and their ship.

The 7,500-ton *Marblehead*, commissioned in 1924 and, as a four-funneled cruiser a rare bird among the newer, modernized Navy types, was with the Asiatic Fleet when Pearl Harbor was attacked. This fleet was a pitifully small assemblage of equally old war vessels. Even added to the Royal Netherlands Navy and British units in eastern waters, the Allied units could scarcely match the Japanese naval might.

Nonetheless the Allies fought heroically, attacking enemy convoys as the foe poured south toward Malaya, Sumatra, Borneo, Java, New Guinea . . .

Off Balikpapan, Borneo, early in 1942, the *Marblehead*, as one of a small force, exacted a heavy toll from a Japanese convoy pushing through the Makassar Straights.

The cruiser sought a repeat performance on the morning of February 4, as another group of enemy merchantmen, transports, and their escorts was sighted at the southern entrance to these same 200-mile-broad straits between Borneo and the Celebes. This time, the Japanese sent waves of bombers to zero in on the *Marblehead*.

Although she could no longer make her original speed of thirty-four knots, her commanding officer, Capt. Arthur G. Robinson, successfully maneuvered the old cruiser for forty-five minutes out of the way of the falling bombs as gunners banged away at the attackers, hitting some of them. Then, with the fourth wave, comprising some seven bombers, the *Marblehead* was hit twice, while a third near-miss opened up her seams underwater.

From aft came the word to the bridge, "Steering gear's gone, sir." The auxiliary apparatus had been ruptured as well.

Afire down by the bow, the *Marblehead* made a wide circle to port as the bombers kept after her. With the decks slippery from oil and water, it was not an easy matter to work the guns, even to move about.

Below decks, although it seemed apparent that the *Marblehead* was about to founder, the crew stuck heroically to the engines while others stuffed collision mats in jagged bulkhead holes. Lt. (jg) Francis G. Blasdel maintained his post as assistant damage control officer in the smoky central station. There he coordinated information as to flooding, counterflooding in an effort to regain some stability.

Before noon the last of the attackers winged away, satisfied that the cruiser was going to sink. Aboard were fifteen dead and thirty-four badly hurt. The galley itself was gone, along with other vital areas, leaving a hungry ship.

When the pumps were unable to keep up with the rising water, a bucket brigade was formed. Thus, with her bow still awash and being steered erratically by the engines, *Marblehead* limped into Tjilatjap on the south coast of Java. She had truly been, as her captain observed, "bombed to hell!"

Here a very few repairs were effected, a makeshift galley hammered out, although her rudder could not be freed. There wasn't even a dock for her. In addition, enemy aircraft ranged daily over the whole area. While the cruiser waited, Tokyo broadcast her "sinking."

Yet, steering by her engines, the propeller on one side alternating with that on the opposite side, the *Marblehead* steamed 2,000 miles west through submarine-infested waters to the large Royal Navy base at Trincomalee, Ceylon. There the rudder was freed although the base was too busy with its own work to effect further repairs.

The *Marblehead*, still unfit to rejoin what was left of the Asiatic Fleet, continued homeward via Durban (4,400 miles south of Ceylon), Port Elizabeth, and Simonstown, South Africa, then crossed the Atlantic to Recife, Brazil. At last, on May 4, exactly three months after her pounding, the "ship that was bombed to hell" steamed into Brooklyn, from the other side of the earth, not fully seaworthy for any portion of her long safari.

Three days later, and the day after the sobering news of the surrender of Corregidor, the Navy informed the nation of the *Marblehead's* feat.

In February 1943 the submarine *Growler* was operating in the wilderness of the Bismarck Archipelago 300 miles east of New Guinea on her fourth war patrol. The captain, a forty-one-year-old Alabaman, Cdr. Howard W. Gilmore, had already sunk 26,000 tons of enemy shipping to win the Navy Cross. (The estimate was probably conservative.)

On the night of February 7, in Steffan Strait, near Watom Island, while on the surface, *Growler* spotted an enemy gunboat of some 2,500 tons boiling through the murk. It was too late to submerge or even swing into position for firing torpedoes. Gilmore, still in the conning tower, shouted down the order: "Left full rudder!"

He would ram.

The collision alarm jangled as watertight doors began to close electrically. The seconds ran out.

With the enemy's guns sweeping the submarine's bridge, *Growler* hurled herself at seventeen knots into the gunboat's port side, opening a gash into which poured a cataract of the dark waters. Below at the periscope eyepiece came Gilmore's order: "Take her down!"

It was the skipper's last command. Along with two junior officers of the deck and one lookout, he was dying from wounds. The order, which some heard as "Clear the bridge!", had to be obeyed if the *Growler* were to be saved. The executive officer, Lt. Cdr. Arnold F. Schade, took her down, a crippled submarine with thirty-five feet of the bow crumpled and bent at right angles, two torpedo tubes too badly bent to be closed.

She submerged, awaiting depth charges. They did not come. After temporary shorings of the *Growler's* forward bulkheads, the exec was able to bring his submarine to the surface. There was no sign of the enemy gunboat.

Crippled as she was, with her conning tower twisted by shells and bullets, the *Growler* made it back. Gilmore became the first submariner to win the Congressional Medal of Honor, posthumously.

"His loss," wrote Adm. William F. Halsey, "will be keenly felt by all who knew him . . . he cannot be replaced."

"Take her down!" has found its place in the United States Navy's lexicon of inspiration.

In October of the same year the submarine *Puffer* was engaged in torpedoing a merchantman in the Makassar Straits near the scene of the *Marblehead's* punishment when she was attacked by a patrol boat of the *Chidori* class. These were comparable to American destroyer escorts and quite effective.

The attack was of exceptional violence. As *Puffer* crash-dived, under emergency orders of her captain, Lt. Cdr. M. J. Jensen, sea water surged in from sprung valves and gaskets, light bulbs popped, and flakes of cork insulation were strewn about like wood chips. The rudder and stern planes, damaged, worked imperfectly.

At more than 200 feet below the surface the *Puffer* continued to be shaken by depth charges. Hour after hour passed, and still she could not elude the enemy patrol craft. After twelve hours of unrelieved tension when each explosion could have been the crew's last, the carbon dioxide absorbent and oxygen had almost been exhausted. The air was dead and foul. The men were bathed in sweat as humid temperatures poked toward 125 degrees.

For about eighteen hours the "ash cans" kept coming down. Then they stopped. Soon, the *Puffer* lost sonar, or listening device contact, with the patrol boat's propellers.

Jensen took no chances, however. He waited until he had been under for thirty-one hours—a record for this depth and these conditions—then surfaced. The crew breathed fresh air like drunken men.

Puffer showed a port list. Her deck gear including the 3-inch gun was a mess. But she ultimately reached Australia. She proved anew that a warship, given the added ingredient of the skill and raw courage of her crew, can defy all the rules to return from the dead.

BIBLIOGRAPHY

These books, among others, were consulted:

Bowman, Lt. Marvin K., USN (with the advice and assistance of Mr. Paul Warrick, of Atlanta, Georgia). *Big Ben the Flat Top, the Story of the USS Franklin.* Atlanta, Albert Love Enterprises, 1946.

Castillo, Capt. Edmund L. *Flat-Tops.* New York, Random House, 1969.

Morison, Samuel E. *Victory in the Pacific,* Vol. XIV. Boston, Little, Brown, & Co., 1960.

O'Callahan, Father Joseph T., S. J. *I Was Chaplain on the Franklin.* New York, The Macmillan Co., 1956.

Picking, Sherwood. *Sea Fight off Monhegan.* Portland, privately printed, 1941.

Polmar, Norman. *Aircraft Carriers.* New York, Doubleday, 1969.

Roscoe, Theodore. *True Tales of Bold Escapes.* Englewood Cliffs, N.J., Prentice-Hall Inc., 1965.

Taylor, Theodore. *The Magnificent Mitscher.* New York, Norton, 1954.

These magazines in particular contained articles concerning the *Franklin: Colliers* (June 23 and June 30, 1945), "Chaplain Courageous," by Quentin Reynolds; and *Our Navy* (February, 1961). Coverage is also to be found in *Life, Newsweek,* and *Time* (May–June, 1945).

These newspapers were consulted: *Atlanta Journal; Baltimore Sun; Boston Globe; Chicago Tribune; Eastern Argus* (Portland, Maine) concerning the *Boxer-Enterprise* battle; *Kansas City Star; Los Angeles Times; Newark Evening News; The New York Times; New York Daily News; Providence Journal; Richmond Times-Dispatch; St. Louis Post-Dispatch; Seattle Times; Washington Post.*

INDEX

The **Naval Institute Press** is the book-publishing arm of the U.S. Naval Institute, a private, nonprofit, membership society for sea service professionals and others who share an interest in naval and maritime affairs. Established in 1873 at the U.S. Naval Academy in Annapolis, Maryland, where its offices remain today, the Naval Institute has members worldwide.

Members of the Naval Institute support the education programs of the society and receive the influential monthly magazine *Proceedings* and discounts on fine nautical prints and on ship and aircraft photos. They also have access to the transcripts of the Institute's Oral History Program and get discounted admission to any of the Institute-sponsored seminars offered around the country.

The Naval Institute also publishes *Naval History* magazine. This colorful bimonthly is filled with entertaining and thought-provoking articles, first-person reminiscences, and dramatic art and photography. Members receive a discount on *Naval History* subscriptions.

The Naval Institute's book-publishing program, begun in 1898 with basic guides to naval practices, has broadened its scope in recent years to include books of more general interest. Now the Naval Institute Press publishes about 100 titles each year, ranging from how-to books on boating and navigation to battle histories, biographies, ship and aircraft guides, and novels. Institute members receive discounts of 20 to 50 percent on the Press's nearly 600 books in print.

Full-time students are eligible for special half-price membership rates. Life memberships are also available.

For a free catalog describing Naval Institute Press books currently available, and for further information about subscribing to *Naval History* magazine or about joining the U.S. Naval Institute, please write to:

Membership Department
U.S. Naval Institute
118 Maryland Avenue
Annapolis, MD 21402-5035
Telephone: (800) 233-8764
Fax: (410) 269-7940
Web address: www.usni.org